THE WORLD AFTER NORMAL:

ESSAYS ON CULTURE, ECONOMICS AND SOCIETY IN A MOMENT OF TRANSFORMATION

ERIC GARLAND

Garland, Eric A. *The World After Normal: Essays on culture and society in a moment of transformation*

ISBN-10: 098355952X

ISBN-13: 978-0-9835595-2-8

Published by Wallingford Press, Saint Louis, Missouri, USA

TABLE OF CONTENTS

MAKING SENSE OF A WORLD AFTER NORMAL

As I write this in January of the year of the Common Era 2013, executives of the world's largest and most influential institutions are meeting in Davos, Switzerland to discuss "the fate of the world." The giddily reported whisperings coming out of the halls of Swarovski crystal and caviar tell us that, "*The global recovery is happening, but it is very, very fragile. The worst, however, is behind us!*" In effect, the crisis is over; things are going back to Normal; your leaders are still in charge; everything is fine; have you seen the new season of American Idol?

Do you buy that? I do not.

You cannot blame these people for attempting to get beyond the interminable sense of uneasiness that came ever since the rotten core of global finance was exposed in 2008. Many Davos participants were perhaps wondering at one point or another if they were going to receive a complimentary pitchfork ride, courtesy of their respective unemployed proletariats. People attending Davos were likely privy to - or actively constructing - the fraudulent putrescence that was the financialized housing bubble. They knew about the fly-by-night mortgage brokers, the intentional deception about the creditworthiness of financial products, the foreclosing on people who didn't even *have* mortgages, the trillions in derivatives, the backroom bailouts. These are the people who knew that Greece was taking on debts it would never repay, just like Portugal and Spain. No doubt, at many a moment, they have wondered if the whole thing would even hold together. It is no wonder why they are eager to declare the past five to ten years a crisis that has returned to Normal. They were probably more scared than you were, and with good reason.

Yet I suspect that while most people are excited to go through their daily lives without some financial reporter running onto the set of the nightly news, naked and screaming THE END IS NIGH!!! REPENT!!!! - the cat is out of the bag, the horse done left the barn. The average person is aware, however vaguely, that the People In Charge aren't really in charge of too much. Regular People, whether in America or France or even Germany (a place where people are very good at being In Charge of things) are regaining a healthy disrespect for those who would claim to be in command of a system of unprecedented complexity. The belief in the concept of Normal is dying away. Things are not normal, and nobody is quite in charge, even though some people are loud and have nice suits and show up on TV quite a bit.

This is the world that I am writing about, that special place where authority figures begin to buckle, where the numbers are shown to be bent, and where new ideas are percolating to the surface. It is a far more interesting place than the sterile corporate PR environment that metastasized after America won the Cold War and Capitalism won at everything. It is a place where your local community is your real asset in this world, where the food is special from place to place, where people keep their regional accents. It is a place where ridiculous things happen with significant frequency. This is a world where the most famous purveyors of wisdom comes out with some of the most obsolete, useless recommendations imaginable. Today, the crazy little ideas that seemed so frivolous in the face of the gigantic global economic monoliths that blocked out the sun in the past twenty years are shown to be the only thing that might lead us to a new prosperity.

The world after Normal is a place where political figures are notable for their sheer entertainment value, if not their comforting leadership. It is a place where the conventional wisdom not only ceases to make sense, it is now the official mindset that got us in the mess.

The world after Normal is a great place for freaks.

And speaking in my capacity as a Card Carrying Freak, I have been having a good time observing and commenting on this new world. The following book is a collection of my essays from the past year or so. They are special to me because they represent my transformation from semi-safe corporate consultant to full-on intellectual combatant. Sometime recently, I lost my ability to self-censor. I drop an F-bomb here or there. I give no quarter to frauds and criminals and the terminally useless. It has cost me some readers and attracted just the right kind of unstable, disreputable social pariahs that I love to call my friends. This new band of rogues, geeks, white hat hackers, double agents and upright warriors for peace and whisky are pushing me to describe this new world where branding is something you do to cattle and PR looks increasingly ridiculous. I am having a good time.

What follows are meditations on what I feel are the territories that most need exploring in the world after Normal. Authority - to whom we should listen above all other opinions - is probably the most common subject, as it is the most broken. Economic transition is another key topic here, as most people are anxious about the fact that the financial promises of yesteryear seem far too ephemeral to ride safely into retirement.

This past year also marked the first time I was ever drawn into making direct commentary on partisan politics, a forbidden territory for Washington DC technocrats like myself. My very first piece "Letter to a future Republican strategist regarding white people" went hyper-viral in a matter of hours, attracting a million readers in six days and earning me some of the most entertaining hate mail I have ever received. (I shall never tire of YOUR A RACIST!) Once this seal was broken, I have found myself venturing into all kinds of social commentary about America, even sacrosanct topics such as college football and guns.

As 2012 was the year I publicly resigned from the consulting world, you will also read some of my commentaries on the problems with institutional management. It is perhaps the highest irony that it was only after trying to burn strategic intelligence to the ground that I found myself writing for Harvard Business Review. Life is funny.

Thank you again for joining me on this bizarre, amusing, very human journey, and strap in.

Eric Garland

Saint Louis, Missouri, USA

January 28, 2013

REFLECTIONS ON AUTHORITY

Are you serious? Should I repeat your ideas when chatting at the water cooler? Can your predictions for the future serve as support for what I suggest my organization ought to do? Must we listen to what you say and do as you command? Those are the litmus tests for *authority*. In the Western world, so many centuries after the heavy intellectual lifting of the Enlightenment, we like to believe that we exist in a pure meritocracy for ideas. In reality, we have a heavily authoritarian society in which who is talking frequently counts much more than what they are saying. This is not necessarily a perverse thing; not all humans are equally talented in an intellectual sense, and some people have more experience than others.

That said, our system of expertise and authority is in need of overhaul. The crises of recent years were a result of listening to a certain group of authority figures, and even after the apparent failure of their ideas, they managed to maintain their positions in society. Ben Bernanke went from being the chairman of the Federal Reserve during the blowing of the housing bubble to...the guy credited with *saving* the economy! CNBC's Jim Cramer and Larry Kudlow went from telling everybody that the banking system was terrific and holy and shouting that housing was doing great just prior to the meltdown of the whole casino to...being *right back in the same place*, touted as financial experts whose insight could help you manage your own retirement account.

The guys who planned the Iraq war in 2002 are still booked on TV shows as sober foreign policy analysts. Larry Summers, who helped engineer the repeal of Glass-Steagall and the failure to regulate over-the-counter derivatives still ended up as a financial advisor in the Obama Administration.

Outside of being named "Eric Garland," what do you have to do to get fired for bad performance? (*Note: I get fired a lot.*) The answer to why our authority figures haven't been defenestrated is hidden in a thicket of myths and cultural quirks. I spent a lot of time exploring why we seem unable to simply listen to people on the quality of their ideas versus the quality of their suits.

TOM FRIEDMAN'S EXTRA FLAT, SUPER CREATIVE, TOTALLY UNLIVABLE WORLD

"The world is really flat, and if you're not special, you should worry, because CEOs can give your job to someone in Bangalore. Morality doesn't enter into to it, since what can be done, will be done, and you can be doing it, or someone will do it to you. But it's OK, because individuals are now the main actors of globalization. When the world becomes completely connected by individuals, we can all go back to small town values. So, to survive in this new world without nation-states or a middle class, just give a little extra – like the diner waitress who put more fruit on my friend's plate. And when you're done, read my new book on how America lost its way – and how to fix it! Goodnight."

I recently witnessed an in-person keynote from the Pulitzer-prize winning, monster-selling author, Thomas Friedman. He was invited to tell an audience of information professionals about the future of globalization based on his early 1980s work about cultural trends in the Middle East and his more recent bestseller *The World is Flat*, which mostly informed the reader that China and India are producing scientists and entrepreneurs despite the fact that they are not American.

Given his stature as a public intellectual, one assumes that many leaders consider Friedman's opinion as useful. If he provides top executives and government officials with the same wisdom he doles out in keynotes, it is in the public's interest to deconstruct his view of the future to see if it is a place in which any of us might really want to live.

Tom, clad in a slacks and a button-down with no tie, opens by informing the audience that his only mistake since his Bush-era publishing megasuccess is that the world is even flatter than he realized. So whatever he was saying in 2003 when he was writing the book, we should just think about how much more it is true today. Because after all, back when he wrote his gem, "Twitter was a sound and Skype was a typo!" Much has changed in this crazy, new, even-flatter world – but he will elucidate the path so that we may make wiser choices. These following themes comprise his view of the future of globalization.

The world is really, really flat now. Tom recaps the story of how he discovered that the world was flat because his cab driver in Hungary had a website for his business. In Magyar, German, and English! And he's not even American, or educated, but he has a website! Wow! And also, it's like that time he talked to a CEO in Bangalore – they have clients all over the world! Indians! With clients! We are informed once again to consider how "flat" this world is, and how Twitter – a service he admits he has no experience with – has made it flatter. Somehow.

CEOs can hire anybody in a flat world. Friedman gets to the heart of the matter when he specifies that flatness means CEOs can hire and fire anyone, anywhere. Only two paths to economic stability remain – do something utterly world-class that enables you to work without needing to connect to your neighbors, or do something completely local that is unreplaceable. For the other 94% of the people involved in the routine operations of the corporate industrial world we just took a century to create – you folks should be worried and get ready to really, really compete.

Be creative, do something extra, and get a liberal arts education! How should you compete with the faceless hordes willing to work for a fifth of your current salary? Tom tells us the story of his wife's best friend's husband who has a law firm called Nixon Peabody in Washington DC. He fired a lot of people after the crash of 2008, but not just the lazybones. They fired people who didn't suggest how to do their work in new ways. Ergo, we should all get liberal arts degrees so that we can be creative and tell our bosses new ways to run their companies – or risk the same termination as the rest of the drones. If you can't innovate processes in a law firm, you can be like this one diner waitress Tom met in Minneapolis who gave him extra fruit when his buddy asked for it.

Individuals are the new actors on the global stage. Cell phones allow us all to connect with Twitter and Facebook, which apparently means that individuals are now the primary actor in globalization. The nation-state, the first actor of globalization, is no match for individuals. Corporations, the newest actors in the global flatness story, are nothing when matched against people power. Why, even the people in Syria have cell phones, and they are rising up this week.

Now that we're all flat actors on the global stage, we can go back to small-town, temple/church/ synagogue family values While it may sound like the rapid decomposition of the institutions that guide a monstrously complex global economy might lead to chaos, fear not – it's time for us to have a bake sale! Everything will be great when we finally get back to the values that made America great, even though now half the town will be unemployed and the other half will be telecommuting for their hyperdemanding companies run by Hungarian cabbies.

What can be done, will be done. So you can be doing it or have it done to you! Friedman concludes with a sentiment first expressed, I believe, by Tony Montana in Scarface. In a world of flatness, there is no morality, no guiding principles, no way to stop the inexorable slide toward a life without the institutions that keep America from looking like scenes from *The Road Warrior*. So get innovating and do something exciting to someone else before they do it to you!

And by the way – Tom's next book is about how America lost its way – and how to fix it! On sale soon!

>>>>>>

If this is the strategic insight of America's top intellectual on globalization, it should surprise none of us that the country has lost its way.

Friedman's thesis about the world being flat may have been interesting in 2003 when Americans were first questioning why the real economic flourishing of the 1990s had stalled – but it is far from accurate now. The world is not "flat" so much that it's just finally competitive at a moment of relative peace and – for the moment -

abundant petroleum. For the greater part of the 20th Century, the United States benefited from some unnatural advantages. Post World War II, European and Asian countries had to spend time and treasure rebuilding critical infrastructure while we turned our military-grade aluminum manufacturing straight into consumer goods. Half the world was in the grips of Soviet communism. The United States and its almighty greenback became unusually good places to put capital compared with other nations. Plus, the sheer size of the Baby Boom generation gave a high-octane demographic boost to nearly every sector of the market, from housing to entertainment to university education. The return of competition from all corners of the globe is more normal than it is exceptional. The real factor in this perception of hypercompetition of recent is that global structures of financial capital are finally more or less unified, geopolitical stability is high, and many countries are attempting to go up the value-chain of manufacturing toward services, which are easier to outsource than agriculture or steel production

That which is indeed exceptional is resulting power shift away from sovereign nations to corporations – decentralized, non-democratic institutions that are gaining leverage over the individuals they employ. Friedman is right, the multinational corporation now has greater flexibility and power than the nation-state in setting the global economic agenda. These organizations now have free rein to race to the bottom in terms of salaries given the mobility Friedman correctly describes. To manage the return to Gilded Age labor markets that spawned a half-century of violent Bolshevik revolutionary upheaval,

Tom tells us to get a liberal arts education, to be creative, and that in the future we'll "create" jobs rather than find them.

This is pure fantasy designed to flatter audiences who love to read books. The greatest job security in the world is reserved for technicians: engineering, information technology, and medicine. The former jobs are required in every field, and the latter is in high demand and low supply wherever there are human bodies. If you want lucrative work, your best bet is still to be a technocrat helping expand the current system. Yet Friedman predicts that there will be sweeping demand for French lit majors willing to "question how things are done and innovate," like at his friend's high-powered lobbyist shop.

Bullshit. First, this nation pumps out legions of anthropology/comparative poetry double majors at an alarming rate (and at many times the cost of degrees that the Boomers received) and they are immediately faced with the reality that they have no marketable skills. The vast majority of them are at the mall working retail as you read this; feel free to ask them all about it. America's youth and their parents have been furiously doubling down on the broken liberal education machine, sending America's total college-related debt from $200 million in 2000 to $1 trillion by just 2010.

Second, Friedman is like many elite males of his generation in his total lack of self-awareness about how his cohort handles being told they are doing things the wrong way. A 24 year-old "job creator" will be committing career suicide by stomping up to his 59 year-old superiors to tell them how to fix their company. His friend, the managing partner of one of the most powerful law firms in America, really wants some newly minted, Twitter-obsessed sociology major restructuring their firms tax advisory practice? I doubt it.

Also wrong is the assertion that the individual is the principle actor in globalization. He expands his 2003 to include Twitter and Facebook by positing that the nation-state pales in comparison to the power of a kid with a cellphone.

Just a few years back Friedman thought quite a bit of the nation-state when he recommended and defended our disastrous war of adventure in Iraq. Back in 2002 and 2003, when he was picking up his third Pulitzer, Tom was very bullish on the power of nation-states to force regime change through military invasion and to bring democracy to an entire region from the top down. Now, one supposes, he would just recommend that American kids could just "friend" most of Iraq on Facebook to get the same desired effect. I couldn't tell you his opinion on this since Friedman makes no mention of the debacle in Iraq when he posits his sweeping views of the changing geopolitical landscape. After all, he did tell us that the only thing he got wrong about the world since 2004 was missing additional flatness – not that his taste for interventionist wars based on pure idealism have been shown to be a gruesome catastrophe.

Is information technology a critical, even unprecedented tool in the coordination of social movements? Absolutely. But this doesn't mean that the individual is somehow in a more powerful position. Nation-states set laws and regulation. They collect taxes under pain of prison.

They maintain their borders through force. They go to war, and in the recent case of the United States, now do so with the equivalent of a Post-It's worth of notice to the electorate. (*"Gone to war with Libya – probably won't use ground troops – will get eggs and bread on way back!"*)

Individuals have recently demonstrated their power to the degree they are willing to organization into groups and hold mass protests, but the advent of this technique was 1910, not 2010. But when nation-states don't want to play any more, they use their toolset – legally sanctioned violence in the name of security. Egypt refrained from these techniques in the early part of the Arab Spring because the United States – a nation-state – has ties with its military officers. Where the state has no leverage – Iran, Syria, Yemen, and Libya – the gloves come off and the individual tends to lose. Maybe we just need to engage the 103rd Twitter Corps, but in the power struggle between countries, companies, and individuals, I'm betting on the first two.

Friedman, though, believes that this nascent people power is going to lead to a very special place – a global renaissance in small town values. We'll go back to our houses of worship and have town hall suppers and all get along. This is a classic piece of Baby Boomer nostalgia when the world they helped create looks dystopic. Small town values, the kinds ascribed by Boomers in these situations, usually date from circa 1955. Of course, in these scenarios, we're not supposed to go back to the actual 1950s – Jim Crow lynchings, Jews and Catholics excluded from country clubs, the House Committee on Un-American Activities. Instead we are going to somehow arrive at a future that looks like the set of Happy Days, replete with walkable neighborhoods, clean children, and church bean suppers.

This is when I begin to wonder if Friedman actually knows anything about small business or small towns. Social life in a small town is entirely a function of its economics. You are dependent on your neighbors for their special services they provide you, and this incentivizes you all to get along. I can't punch Frank in the nose at the town tavern, because if I do, that's the last time he'll be fixing my roof. And Frank had better not make a pass at my wife, or he'll be *persona non grata* at my general store forever more, and he can walk ten miles each way to get milk.

This world, I might add, is not heaven – it can even be a bit cold and Sartresque in its begrudging codependence. But it works, as it has for the past five to ten thousand years.

Friedman is describing the inevitability of a world in which the exact opposite social structure will be in place. In his kingdom of flatness, individuals will live in a fractured world in which a few can plug into the global corporate talent pool, a few provide local services of plumbing, day care and haircuts, the rest work for local branches of international franchises – but none of us truly need each other to make our daily bread. This will in no way lead to the mythical land of sweet smiling interdependence, but of people whose allegiances are to everyone but their neighbors. The people in your town become – as they have for so many in America – just another car in traffic, just another cart in front of you in the grocery line, obstacles and not resources.

Also, it should be said that it is pretty cheeky for a man married to the heiress of a fortune made creating strip malls to tell us that we're going to get back to cute little downtowns and warm local interactions. No doubt he benefits mightily from the economic value derived from destroying that very thing over the last fifty years.

Throughout his speech, Friedman intones that "what can be done, will be done." For a man who makes such lip service to the power of individual will, he uses his authority to tell audiences that if they don't like what this world sounds like, too bad. The very institutions that gave structure to his life – community, rule of law, accountability of the powerful to a local population, economic opportunity irrespective of family background – will be evaporating, and you had just better get used to it. Sorry, Gen X and Y. You'll be simultaneously responsible for financing Boomer healthcare entitlements through your nation-state, while seeking employment from global companies that would just as soon hire cheaper labor in dozens of other nations – but I guess that's just the way it goes. Don't waste time discussing the implications of these unprecedented social evolutions. Don't consider different national economic policies. Don't rally your neighbors against what sounds like a dystopia. Just get creative and stuff. This is the height of nihilism since the world he is forecasting is horrible for almost everybody but he and his wife, safely ensconced in their 11,000 square foot mansion in Bethesda.

Friedman stepped forward into the public consciousness in the early eighties to describe the evolution of the Islamic world in the midst of U.S. and Soviet gamesmanship and brought to light a culture and mindset that would ultimately cause an outsized effect on the world around it. His analysis was insightful and compelling. His work succeeded based on its merits. He should be content with his past.

His view of the future, however, is a rehash of poorly examined assumptions delivered by a man completely disconnected from reality.

THE COMING BUBBLE OF OBSOLETE ADVICE

Last week I read a piece in Forbes about how young people today should not complain about "underemployment," the phenomenon of working part-time or at a job unsuited to one's level of education. Instead, says the author, young people should be completely excited to work at minimum wage for an indefinite period of time, to take whatever they can get. The article, helpfully titled Get Over It!, restates, for those who have never heard the myth, that in America you just need to work hard and make your own luck, even if you are starting out with five or ten times as much debt as previous generations.

Today, the nationally-syndicated voice of the mid-20th century, Cal Thomas, tells young people that student debt – which quintupled in America during the last decade, from $200 billion to over a trillion – is really just their personal choice. So young people ought to just *stop* going into debt for college so much, says a man who went to American University when its tuition was around $1200 per year.

Last year, I got to hear the truly inimitable Thomas Friedman tell a live audience that since CEOs can now give your job to "anybody," you should study liberal arts, tell the CEO what he's doing wrong and invent your own job. This will ultimately lead to small town values and prosperity, according to Friedman.

This advice is nonsensical, useless, and if you are in the position of coming out of school as an indebted young person, totally insulting. Rather than indulge the understandable phenomenon of becoming angry at the arrogance and cluelessness of these individuals, I would like to explore is **why** this is happening. We need to understand the psychological mechanism behind the cognitive failure of our elite opinion makers, because I submit that we will be experiencing much more of it in the years to come. We are entering into a bubble of obsolete advice.

America is experiencing a decoupling of its *current experience* from its *past performance*. The America that formed the ideology of its current leadership was one of *growth* in every dimension – growth of population, growth of productivity, growth of land use, growth of total amount of retail square footage per consumer, growth of incomes and, of course, growth of indebtedness. The America of today is defined by the ***end*** of that growth. The generation following the Boomers is half its size, 35 million to their parents' 70 million. The suburbs cannot grow any more, and the exurbs are already beginning to collapse under the cost of its infrastructure, unsupported as it is by a tax-base corroded by the implosion of the subprime mortgage market. Retail square footage is shrinking. Wages are stagnant, and debts are incurred to their maximum to make up the difference. With Boomers still delaying their retirements to extend the hope of reaching the dream lifestyle promised to them by the Wall-Street-401(k)-Industrial-Complex, jobs are few. Thus, new household formation is also collapsing, since kids going back to school for billions of dollars worth of degrees are rarely in a financial position to start families.

The major media of the world is doing its best to mischaracterize this grand transformation by pointing to the banking collapse of 2008, calling that moment a "recession" and this moment a "recovery." It is neither. But the recognition of the major changes I described above would be far too disturbing for the sponsors of those media outlets. To effectively sell their products, advertisers must also sell a story to consumers about a grand narrative, one of stability, comfort and entitlement. We don't just buy paper towels or cars, we also buy the low body fat and comfortable expressions of the mannequins appearing in the advertisements. Accurately describing the end of the consumer lifestyle does not fit well with the demands of the sponsors.

Which brings us to the opinion makers also appearing in such media. These people are in the societal position of writing down their opinions, which are presumably more insightful than those of the guy at your deli making you a sandwich. Ostensibly, these people have technical expertise about how the world works, which qualifies them to hand out their observations in national media. But the world that produced Friedman and Thomas no longer exists. Their expertise and their insight have become completely obsolete. Rather than admit that they no longer possess relevant expertise and set themselves to being curious about the future, these writers are choosing to express advice from a bygone age, one in which they still possess authority. To do otherwise would be far too personally painful. And to a majority of their audience, which formed its ideology in an America than no longer exists, hearing the old myths repeated brings comfort. After all, in the America of the 20th Century, a solid work ethic and an education *was* enough to bring most people a career that would provide a lifestyle filled with the goods and services of the Middle Class. It was a good system, and it attracted the attention of the world. Who wouldn't want to go back to that land, however mythical, in their mind?

In fact, the more disturbing the news gets, and the less relevant the old myths are to the current and future situation, the more we will be hearing obsolete advice. And like a medicine man who shouts ever-louder at the heavens as the clouds no longer obey his commands, so will the counsel of our elites become more shrill, strident and hallucinatory. The vast majority of professional intellectuals from the *ancien regime* will not take kindly to sliding down the societal pyramid toward the level where merely having an opinion guarantees neither income nor notoriety. So we will be the beneficiaries of even more essays about how today's youth are spoiled; how they should be starting families; how we must rekindle consumer confidence; how it was tough for Boomers too, you know. And this will have an audience that will be much more significant than the quality of the work will justify.

What will remain will be many questions. We have yet to find the answers. How we go about that process will define the society which is about to emerge. It will be difficult. And for those already fatigued of considering such difficult questions, there will be an ample market in palliative advice from years gone by. I simply hope that people can tune out this noise when they search for answers that are more relevant to their future.

JONAH LEHRER, MALCOLM GLADWELL AND OUR THIRST FOR NON-THREATENING ANSWERS

This week marked another PR disaster for writer Jonah Lehrer, the intellectual prodigy who has become a best-selling author for his books Proust Was a Neuroscientist, How We Decide and most recently Imagine: How Creativity Works. A few weeks back, Lehrer came under fire for recycling some of his past work in his new job as a staff writer for *The New Yorker*. This past week, he admitted that he fabricated quotes attributed to Bob Dylan in his latest book, and has subsequently resigned from the magazine all together. One thing is clear – when you get the most cherry gig in all of English-language journalism at age 31, you should expect that more than a few people may be fact-checking you in hopes of taking you down a notch. But I am not here to hogpile on a young man who is no doubt feeling the weight of the world on his shoulders right now. Quick success can be as much of a curse as it is a blessing, and while such amateur errors seem out of character, we cannot know what is going through someone's head as they take on a heavy cultural mantle of being expected to provide exceptional wisdom day in and day out.

I am more interested in why such awesome commercial success has been thrust on Lehrer and his publishing industry forebear, Malcolm Gladwell, author of the galactic best sellers *The Tipping Point, Blink, and Outliers*. In full disclosure, I am in their same business of providing nonfiction insights about the world around us, and every analysis I provide should be filtered for possible jealousy or self-consciousness. Regardless, I believe that the enormity of their success says as much about Western industrial economies and our culture as it does about their skills as public intellectuals.

Let us be clear – both Lehrer and Gladwell are worthy authors. Both write with tremendous fluidity and a gift for turning complex situations into engaging narratives. They are both excellent thinkers and world-class writers, period. But step back and look at the topics they cover:

- How trends emerge in the global economy
- How we make decisions
- How people are creative
- How people achieve success

Neither Gladwell nor Lehrer attempt to cover single subjects with both breadth and depth, like, for example, Mark Kurlansky does in Salt and Cod. They swing for the fences and attempt to explain how "things happen" or "how brains work." They mix together enormous fields that are still in their infancy, such as neuroscience, with popular fields like art and music and sports. In works of less than 500 pages, Gladwell and Lehrer attempt to enlighten the reader on How the World Works, What People are Really Like, and How Greatness Happens without getting into any of the technical details that would absolutely overwhelm the majority of the readers traipsing through airport book shop before grabbing their flight home.

The incredible complexity of neurotransmitters, global supply chains, or police emergency response training is smoothed over, edited, reduced to a light and palatable narrative of someone with the speech pattern of an Ivy League education. More than actionable insights, this kind of popular analysis gives the reader something far more immediately valuable – the *feeling that they have a sophisticated view of the world.* Reading this kind of book, the sharp corners, uncomfortable realizations, insecurity, class struggle and information overload of the early 21st century is massaged away into a single comfortable feeling - *our elites know what is going on, and the complexity of the world can be explained in a calm, hip, erudite way.*

We fall in love with "interesting" explanations

It is no coincidence that this kind of book achieved its apex just as Dot Com One began to crash, and America's bubble and war economies thrived in earnest against a backdrop of terrorism, job outsourcing and economic uncertainty. *The Tipping Point* emerged in the year 2000, at the height of mendacity of Dot Com One, just prior to the unveiling of the crimes of Enron, Global Crossing and the rest of their cohort who exemplified the excesses of fraudulent accounting and pure grift. And if you recall, even that which wasn't pure fraud was still pretty weird – this was the era of Pets.com, "worth $4 billion but searching for a business model," leased Porsche Boxsters, getting paid $60,000 to spell HTML, and other epic tomfoolery. The world was having a great time, but nothing made a whole lot of sense.

Into this void of strangeness steps journalist Malcolm Gladwell, looking smart yet left-of-center with his trademark 'fro and casual business dress. Nothing makes sense, but he could show you how trends emerge from *mavens* and *connectors* and Williamsburg, Brooklyn. He talks in code, discussing The Law of the Few, The Stickiness Factor, and The Power of Context. Instead of citing General Electric or Sony, he references *Sesame Street*'s Elmo and Nickelodeon's *Blue's Clues*.

Marketing people go berserk – here is a theory that will help them aim their giant budgets with the goal of hitting a "tipping point." CEOs love the book because it explains "we're in a brand new world" requiring "new strategies." People in Brooklyn love the book because, well, it makes Brooklyn out to be important. MBA students, journalists, homemakers, bowlers, and for **years** pretty much every other literate person in the Anglo-Saxon world buys both a hardcover and softcover version. Gladwell makes enough money to live in his own ziggurat and travel the world in a golden sleigh drawn by a team of unicorns. All this because the book is *perfect* – it arrives at a time that the American model of economic growth is beginning to falter, and nobody is ready to look at the real problems. This type of intellectual material arrives as the perfect placeholder until the world is forced to consider that which could be inconvenient and ugly.

And soon after, while *Tipping Point* is still selling pallet loads every nine seconds, the terrorist attacks of September 11, 2001 occur. In terms of absolute damage, it is a relatively small loss of life and property; despite the trauma, Americans continue to have reliable food supply, electricity, fuel and the basics of life. But the intellectual damage is catastrophic. For the years ahead, America will be unable to think rationally about its future, too busy jumping at shadows, launching wars of adventure, deepening its political divide, mocking dissent, and too busy relying on mythology to wisely assess and implement anything that looks like a coherent plan.

America splits its valuable time between blowing an enormously obvious housing bubble, demanding Master's degrees for entry-level positions, and badly managing the bloodbaths of Iraq and Afghanistan. Still desirous of wisdom about the world around us, the buying public turns to Gladwell's smash sophomore hit – *Blink: The Power of Thinking Without Thinking*, which is an outstanding title given the intellectual environment. Gladwell takes his reader into "the connection between cutting-edge psychological and neurological research and human intuition," focusing on how real decisions happen while bypassing our conscious powers of reason. This is a perfect message for the current environment, since from the presidential administration on down, America has by this time developed a deep and abiding mistrust of anyone actively engaging their capacity for logic instead of bowing down to the hyperbolic expansion of banks, military budgets or secret government surveillance regimes.

Eventually, Gladwell turns to another blockbuster topic with *Outliers*- how really talented, rich and famous people got really talented, rich and famous, which dovetails nicely with our burgeoning national obsession with the Hiltons and Kardashians. The book also complements the emerging reality that becoming prosperous simply by getting a public education and doing a good job is becoming nigh-on impossible.

The perfect books for a culture avoiding real problems

Taken together all three of these books form a pattern when set against the backdrop of the major trends changing the United States, Europe, ascendant Asia, and indeed the whole world. **The analyses proposed by Gladwell, and later continued by Lehrer, skate over the top of any of the real problems facing humanity, remaining on the surface of consumer and business trends without taking any kind of an empathetic look at what real people are experiencing.** Their books are perfect expressions of the elite class that is running the world, since the concerns of the elite tend to be hermetically sealed from any of the problems of the middle or lower classes, whose troubles are being amplified as the 21st century grinds on.

In America, fewer people are covered by health insurance than in 2000 – but you won't find those concerns in books on "how we make tough decisions super quick." In the time since *The Tipping Point* came out, student loan debt has quintupled in the US alone, saddling people from age 20 to 65 with loans they may never eliminate entirely.

Outliers rehashes the Buddhist notion of spending 10,000 hours on a livelihood, but certainly doesn't waste time sweating about how to have a crack at success is going to mean more risk of personal bankruptcy than ever before. The suburban pattern of development is proving to be a complete disaster for our collective futures, as we have both peak oil and trillions of dollars of housing bubbles still facing us.

Don't bother looking for that set of decisions in any books that talk about how Marcel Proust thought of the thematics of neurolinguistic romanticism in *Du côté de Chez Swann*. And in the decade where many of our democratic institutions seemed to fold in the face of torture regimes and central bank Ponzi schemes, we avoided looking at the actual way "trends" emerge through policy decisions behind closed doors in favor of "mavens" and "connectors" in "hip neighborhoods." Never mind the actual power structure of the world, let's focus on hipsters.

These intellectual contributions were the perfect complement to the power structure of the last decade, in which all too many senior executives have abdicated leadership in favor of fleecing many of the institutions they were sworn to protect. Dealing with discomfort, honest self-analysis instead of shallow, pseudo-scientific reflections on "the brain," speaking truth to power, enforcing checks and balances – these things have all been out of fashion in a world where we worship power and forget the trials of history. It should be no surprise that we buy millions of copies of books that let us go through the motions of thinking about civilization without any of the challenges that any useful idea will force on us.

Returning to the plight of Jonah Lehrer, I cannot say I'm surprised that he seems to have made some unforced errors as he sits atop the world of journalism at age thirty-one. Perhaps he no longer wants to play this game. He will be inheriting the world that this type of thinking creates. The world expects regular insight from him, and if he is as smart as he appears, he might not be able to play this game with a straight face much longer. Perhaps Lehrer will be back with some real material, and instead of blathering about Bob Dylan, he will be examining how we can alleviate poverty in crumbling American cities. It won't be as hip or as clean, but maybe he will be able to sleep at night.

JONAH LEHRER, FAREED ZAKARIA, AND OUR LOVE OF AUTHORITY OVER CONTENT

I am sad to see Fareed Zakaria join the recent spate of top journalists to be exposed for practicing plagiarism in their work in major media. He has been one of the most insightful thinkers on geopolitics to grace the television and his work seems blessedly free of the ideological distortions of much of the foreign policy community in the United States. Still, he is clearly not immune from the shortcuts to which big name journalists can fall victim.

I don't want to cover Zakaria's failure – let Time magazine and the media buying public work on that issue. Instead, I would like to cover what Jonah Lehrer and Zakaria have in common, and the much more troubling psychological issues that lead to such professional failings.

Authority is power, and power corrupts

We live in a very authoritarian world today, but particularly in the United States, a country that is supposed to be built around not trusting central power. Still, the average person today has an unattractive habit of genuflecting to position, meritocratic or inherited. For a Western culture that is supposed to have thrown off the chains of feudalism and divine right of kings some centuries ago, title and position inspire deference in a great number of people. Those who are rich are assumed to be business savvy and deserving of their wealth. Military leaders are assumed to be competent and brave. Media figures are assumed to be wise, possessing some great capability in logic and insight. Economic policy makers – say, Ben Bernanke – are presumed to understand the macroeconomic system in which they make policy, and to improve people's lives. Doctors are assumed to be up to date on all medical literature and dispensing advice based on evidence that supports their standard of care. This is not to say that such preconceived notions are *a priori* incorrect, but rather to point out that we give people with position a significant amount of benefit of the doubt. In Western society right now, position confers authority.

In the intellectual world, finally getting some authority, usually by selling a lot of copies of something, means your life will change. For one thing, you will be paid for your intellectual efforts, possibly a quite lavish rate of remuneration if you are on international media a lot. You will be invited to dinner parties and conferences. You will be invited to speak at universities, possibly teach. And no doubt, when you wish to write opinion columns, you may be given a spotlight in media that goes out to millions of people. Everything you write will be taken more seriously than if you were "a nobody."

Seduced by laziness, drawn to their own destruction

I'm going call the following idea the **Garland Authority/Content Ratio**, which states that the average media consumer in Western society pays 90% attention to who is talking, and 10% to what they say. This is clearly unscientific, but just go with me. Authority is so important and critical thinking is so scarce that when the vast, vast majority of people see something on TV, in print, or on the Internet, they ask, "Well, who's talking?" If the name and the face resonate, then they skim some of what that person is saying, and a meme is born, an idea transferred. If the speaker is unknown to them, then chances of that idea being propagated is significantly reduced. Basically, the majority of audiences cannot digest the information set before them, so they rely on authority to save time and energy.

Yes, this is how we end up going to war in Iraq and giving bankers bonuses straight out of the federal treasury. But I digress.

Once you are a Major Media Figure, you can relax considerably. You can write some straight up nonsense and still have people scratch their beards and think deeply about whatever dribbled out of your brain. You can restate old ideas as if they were new. You assert opinions without worrying about showing ample evidence, the way a less-authoritative speaker would.

This relaxation can go too far. Lehrer and Zakaria have found this out the hard way. They have gone a step too far, instead of stealing ideas from other people – which happens all the time, probably a positive thing in an active culture – to stealing *verbatim paragraphs*. They go from making assertions without evidence to just inventing quotes entirely. The intoxicating power of authority has weakened the connection between excellent work and excellent outcome, and finally a rupture occurred that was big enough for everybody to notice.

Oh, there is plenty of dirty laundry in the world of public intellectuals. I wonder what would happen if it became public just how many of your favorite smarty-pantses use ghost writers. Or if it came to light how many big names are stealing from their students and lesser known colleagues, knowing they would never get caught, as their "citation" would be in a much bigger public arena first. The power of authority leads to a plantation type dynamic, in which the people holding position deriving economic advantage from the efforts of the ignored and underpaid.

Hopefully this string of journalistic scandals will teach everybody to read more carefully, to pay attention to what is written much more than who is doing the writing.

AUTHOR SCANDALS AND THE OVERDUE COLLAPSE OF THE AUTHORITY-MEDIA COMPLEX

For several weeks now, I have been writing and giving interviews about why so many best-selling "thought leader"-type authors are falling from grace all at once. My thesis is that they all tend to be held up not uniquely by merit, but by a consolidated media environment that confers authority on them, often to the exclusion of many other voices. Moreover, the ascent of decreasingly rigorous thought leaders is likely due in part to our psychological dependence on authority figures in times of fearful uncertainty – the kind we have had since Dot Com One imploded, 9/11 occurred, and the financial system nearly self-destructed in 2008.

In the following piece, I'd like to take the reader through the last few decades of intellectual life from my unusual point of view as an author trying to make it in the "thought leader" world, as a professional analyst serving executives in business and government, and as a resident of Washington DC during this significant and often disturbing transition.

I am taking a Gladwellian trip down memory lane here to show a narrative you may not have considered. (Ironic, I know.) Unlike some of the people recently crucified, I'm not here to call this definitively true, complete or scientifically provable. Unlike some of our recent fallen authority figures, I'm not going to pretend that a few pages of narrative and anecdote is enough to digest the psychology of authority in the last few decades. But I think when you see the business of author-speaker-TV personality in the context of a decade rife with psychological trauma and sheer incompetence, the sudden defenestration of a certain class of experts makes much more sense.

Far beyond the story of a few overpaid writers jeopardizing their gigs in the media, we are at a turning point in American culture in which we collectively move past a painful loss of innocence and regain our ability to critically evaluate our future and who should lead it. This story arcs from naiveté, to disillusionment, to maturity. America lost the exuberant bloom that came from decades of economic success and cultural preeminence in a rapid turn of events that saw self-confidence and a sense of safety ripped away from its people. To regain that confidence, the people turned to false authority figures in a vain attempt to regain what was lost. But don't worry – it may all have a happy ending.

The sudden collapse of well-manicured authority figures

It was the Bob Dylan quote forgery heard 'round the world. Jonah Lehrer, a best-selling author for his books explaining the implications of neuroscience research to regular folks, fell from grace in a few short weeks as two scandals emerged in rapid succession. First was the charge that he was recycling his own old material from other publications in his new column at *The New Yorker*. This was really a matter for his publisher and the few avid readers who noticed the redundancy, but it was followed quickly by the revelation of his invented quote from Bob Dylan. Now, Lehrer was brought to task by every journalist, editor and intellectual worker with an Internet connection. His resignation from *The New Yorker* followed, leaving people to scratch their heads in wonder about how somebody with so much caché could fall from grace so quickly by such obvious professional failings.

This of course was not the end for mediagenic thought leaders falling into disrepute. Fareed Zakaria was discovered to be either lifting quotes from a Harvard professor, or employing a ghostwriter who did the same. Not long after his suspension, Zakaria was soon joined by his colleague Niall Ferguson, British historian, TV host, and Harvard professor, who starred on the cover of Newsweek with an essay pleading for the replacement of Barack Obama using selective quotes from the Congressional Budget Office and statistics that surreptitiously blamed the president for job losses that began in earnest under his predecessor. The Scottish historian (curiously referring to the U.S. Republican party as "his team" despite not being a citizen eligible to vote) was pilloried in various publications, not so much for his political views, but for reasoning and prose so poor he would likely give it a failing grade if he received it from one of his students.

For my part, I wrote an essay entitled, "Jonah Lehrer, Malcolm Gladwell and our thirst for non-threatening answers" which went on to be picked up around the Web, engendering quite a bit of conversation. The essay ultimately encouraged a group of PhD scientists to seize on the moment and take Gladwell to task for cheapening the rigor of their profession in the quest for book sales. This surprisingly motivated Gladwell to actually defend himself in the comments section of the blog, revealing some pent-up animosity between the world-famous science writer and the people in the real trenches of scientific research who feel that their discipline is given short shrift in his brand of publishing.

All of this happened within a few weeks. What the blue blazes is going on here? Why is such skepticism bubbling to the surface so quickly?

The thought leadership game in the post-Soviet era

To put these events into context, we should take a broader view of the business of thought leadership – that is, selling books and giving speeches for money. By way of caveat, this is my business model as well, so I beg the reader to scour every one of my assertions for jealousy and sour grapes. One cannot be in the business of asking for rigorous analysis without expecting it heaped on oneself.

So then, let us go back all the way to the 1990s. Grunge bands roamed the Earth, The Internet was considered strange by all but a few computer nerds, and Europe had sixteen different currencies. China was still a place "that Nixon opened up," and we had barely stopped seeing Japan as the economic powerhouse of tomorrow. This period of technological innovation and economic expansion was really marked by the peaceable end of the Cold War, and America's ascendance to hegemonic power.

The United States had been counterbalanced in terms of its economic system and political philosophy all around the world by Russian communism. Plenty of nations, from Cuba to Czechoslovakia to Vietnam chose (or were coerced into) the Soviet communist system, in stark contrast to the beliefs and techniques of Western business and government.

And lest ye forget that communism didn't ever work out, have a gander at one of my favorite books on futurism, *To the Year 2000*, written by a Western German economist in 1960 who forecast that capitalism might lose to communism by the turn of the millennium because the Soviet Union had markedly better *machine tools*, which were the reason for its success. For a while there, communism appeared to be giving Western capitalism a run for its money, in economic success if not individual freedom. So when the Commies melted down in 1991, it was a huge victory over an ideological foe which only looks inevitable in retrospect.

This created a boom market for American business ideas. For consultancies, life could not have been any better. Entire countries were paying U.S. consulting firms to come in and show them how *generally accepted accounting principles* might function in a place where you put the cash from the till in your pocket at the end of every night. Places that had centrally planned economies were thirsty for the American managerial techniques of *marketing*, a strange sorcery by which you asked people what they wanted, and then made some credible plan to give it to them. But how to give it to them with some degree of quality? America exported lessons learned during its long history of manufacturing, not to mention its innovative quality assurance methods such as Motorola's *Six Sigma*. America's robust business in thought leadership could be summed up by "*Hey guys, this is how we got so rich – want to learn how to do it yourselves?*"

Let us look at the kinds of books that flourished in such an environment. The majority of bestsellers were fairly simple explanations of *management techniques that worked.* Why were these authoritative? Because the theories and applications in the books were derived from existing success stories which could be easily verified. Take the 1994 book *Built to Last*, by Jim Collins and Jerry Porras. It described why some companies did great and others did less great. You read the book and you learn how Proctor & Gamble out competed Colgate, why Motorola bested Zenith and other examples that you verify by looking at the companies' annual reports. *These are the big winners in a country full of winners – want to know how they do it? Here.* And so titles of this sort filled up business book stores from New York to Bratislava, from Johannesburg to Shanghai, translating American "best practices" into dozens of languages.

Back in those days you had mega-sellers like The Seven Habits of Highly Effective People (1990). Effective Hungarian chefs? Effective Mongolian horsemen? Effective Indian yogis? No, dude – *effective American executives.* Who are stinking rich while your whole country has only four working air conditioning units at any given time, and has a currency backed by lumps of tungsten that depreciates 9% every eight hours. Effective = American business guys and the habits that have made them rich.

Other mega-titles of the era include The E-Myth (1985), which tears apart the techniques of the artisan one-man shop in favor of franchising. In your little town, you have some guy who makes great pizza – so what? He works sixteen hours a day and never takes a vacation. We have Domino's and Pizza Hut, and the guys who own those franchises spent their days feeding polo ponies, not slaving over some stove. We'll show you how to get your dream into every mini-mall in whatever country it is you come from. (*You do have mini-malls, right?*) What's our proof it works? Just look at America, dude!

You can go on and on looking at titles from the 1980s and 90s that show *how to do things*. From accounting to human resources, any author who could explain the fine points of American bureaucracy was due a decent book advance, a few royalty checks, and a shot at opening a consultancy that could bring these proven techniques to the parts of the world that had not received such wisdom, whether Tuscaloosa or Timbuktu. Your insights did not need to be earth-shattering since the American system itself was plenty impressive on its own.

The end of the party

By the end of the 1990s, the era of failsafe American business practices was about to come to a screeching halt. Sure, by the late nineties, things were positively thrumming throughout the economic world. We were enjoying a full decade of the Soviet menace slowly decomposing without a single nuclear exchange – a pleasant surprise in a world were empires do not usually go quietly or peacefully. China was opening up, spurring American execs to wonder aloud "if we could only get 2% of their market!" Europe was reintegrating the states it lost to the Iron Curtain. Wonder of wonders, even Vietnam and Cambodia were reentering the world system. And Americans, clever innovators they were, looked to capitalize on past successes with this thing called The Internet and all that it enabled. Times were good.

As the 1990s went on, the manic excitement about American business practices led to some unusual decisions. Since the Reagan Era, businesses were clamoring for the government to take supposedly onerous regulation off their backs. *We're doing so well, imagine if we could really unleash our ideas on the world without meddlesome functionaries always asking for paperwork and proof of meeting arbitrary standards.* Curiously, this mindset thundered ahead well after the Reagan and Bush White Houses. Critically, there was ample pressure to lower the artificial barriers keeping media companies from consolidating into empires. Lobbyists wheedled and cajoled so that single companies could roll up radio, newspapers, record labels, publishing houses and TV from coast to coast and around the world. More on that later.

Finance saw another great push to relax the rules of the game which had been, ironically, serving America extremely well for decades. A couple of Bill Clinton's apparatchiks, Larry Summers and Robert Rubin, took aim at legislation such as *Glass-Steagall*, which kept risk-seeking investment banks and stability-promising commercial banks from repeating the antics of the Great Depression. Also in the sight of these economic luminaries who split their time between Wall Street and Washington was the goal of removing government oversight from a new "innovative" American financial instrument, *derivatives*, which include strangely named products such as *credit default swaps* and *collateralized debt obligations*.

Deregulation was a done deal. After all, how could the bulletproof set of American "best practices" steer us wrong. If it's Americans doing it, *clearly it's the best*.

Or the *bust*. After a few years of what Ayn Randian monetarist Alan Greenspan insufficiently dubbed "irrational exuberance," all hell broke loose in American business. We believed so much in our vaunted capital allocation practices on Wall Street that investors everywhere credulously poured money into ePetWalkers.com, SpatulaWarehouse.net, not to mention PickABuzzwordAndHaveAnIPO.com. These innovators were "still searching for a business model," but the analysts – the ones down the hall from the guys who sold you the stock – believed that these companies could possibly break out, Pets.com style!

At the same moment, business magazines were all aflutter over the hard-business side of the Dot Com Era, an innovative powerhouse called Enron. Whereas your company perhaps did trifling Old Economy things such as buy products at a low price and sell them at a higher price, Enron was way, way more sophisticated. It *created markets*, and *created efficiencies* and *wheeled energy futures*, or something – but it was based in Texas, where everyone in the company, from Ken Lay on down, made scads of loot and owned fancy cars.

It turned out, that while America exported its successful model of finance and accounting to the rest of the world, it kept, um, *innovating* at home, creating brand new practices that were based on wishful thinking at best, and utter fraud at worst. A huge portion of the Nasdaq was declared worthless, with only a few deserving candidates such as Amazon and EBay escaping the bloodbath. And the genius financiers at Enron were of course discovered to have been keeping their books solvent only by lending money to fictional companies in long-forgotten Caribbean islands and calling it "revenue." The American model of business management, for the first time in a long time, was under threat from internal failings rather than external enemies. This was a blow to the entire American psyche, and it was a foreign feeling.

The rise of alternate theories in an alternate universe

Just prior to the end of Dot Com exuberance came a new sort of book emanating from a thoughtful and eloquent journalist from the *Washington Post* and *The New Yorker* by the name of Malcolm Gladwell. Rather than rehash received wisdom from successful functionaries, Gladwell turned to unusual explanations for chaotic-seeming events. He wrote a book called *The Tipping Point* which went on to a phenomenal success for describing an alternate vision of how phenomena appear in complex societies, which mimicked, say, viruses in complex biological ecosystems rather than turgid, linear corporate mechanistics. Gladwell's explanations were far from rigorous or complete, but they offered a glimmer of hope that if you could understand chaos; perhaps you could control it, or at least use it to your advantage. You couldn't learn about marketing products in the Internet age through something like like a marketing textbook, but maybe you stood a shot at learning how to be a *maven* or a *connector*.

This, it turned out, was perfectly timed for an era in which conventional explanations seemed to offer little comfort. After all, American business assumptions were under threat. And little did we know that all of our assumptions were soon to follow.

>>>>>>>>>

So much has been said already about the implications of that gorgeous fall day on the East Coast of the United States, September the 11th, 2001. Not enough has been said about the psychological implications.

The immediate aftermath was one centered around practicality. The United States set itself to excavating the crater in lower Manhattan and covering the gigantic hole in the Pentagon, along with clearing debris in Pennsylvania from a fallen aircraft. The names of the dead were tallied. In places like the New York metropolitan area, hundreds upon hundreds of funerals needed to be scheduled in a staggered pattern, so that people who knew multiple of the slain in a single company at the World Trade Center could pay their respects with individual attention.

After the initial shock wore off, the dead buried, and the damage cleared, there was the matter of *what do we do next*? And this is where life changed permanently, for America and for the world. The people of the United States were fundamentally without a compass, having had the comforting assumptions of their own competence ripped away, and they sought authority wherever they could find it. Before, success came with its own built-in authority. Now, the authority Americans so desperately missed had to be imposed from the top down. Serendipitously, the occupants of the White House, George W. Bush and Dick Cheney, were all too pleased to project that very authority from the institution they currently occupied. First they told Americans to go shopping. Naturally, they had other plans, too.

America went to war. Americans knew that if one thing was still left functioning, it was their well-funded military machine. The U.S. intelligence community had traced the terrorist operation back to the nation-state of Afghanistan, whose rogue Taliban government had been housing the group which appeared to be responsible for the attacks. They were religious extremists, which really came as no surprise to American intelligence, which had been paying them for that exact reason to fight the Soviets in Afghanistan just a few decades earlier. But clearly this group had metastasized into a threat to the U.S. homeland. For those watching the horrific antics of the Taliban prior to September 11 – stoning women to death, hanging televisions (?) and firing missiles at millennia-old statues of the Buddha – it seemed rational to send the US military to deal with the situation. All parts of the military, from active duty branches to the CIA received hundreds of thousands of enlistees looking to take part in this new national project. The national narrative was still quite coherent.

The alternate universe began in earnest on January 29, 2002 with George W. Bush's State of the Union speech. America was anxious to hear an update on its military action in Afghanistan, but heard so much more. This speech was a harbinger of what was to become of American intellectual culture. President Bush informed the American people not only of its military victory over the Afghan regime, but of its much broader plan for what it would call "security." Bush trumpeted that the enemies we captured in Afghanistan were now in a place called "Guantanamo Bay," a small base America "possessed" in the country of Cuba, of all places. He gave ample warning about the future intentions of America's military machine with a description of North Korean, Iranian, and Iraqi regimes as an "axis of evil" bent on, among other things, threatening the world with *weapons of mass destruction*, a phrase that would feature prominently in the years to come. America was being told that this new plan for its security had leapt over from the mission to destroy the al-Qaeda network, to direct aggression against nation-states with unfriendly regimes. Moreover, the mission now seemed to have a totally global focus, securing all countries everywhere against "thousands" of trained killers. While these ideas did not necessarily follow, America had come to rely on the authority of its military, intelligence and executive branch in these matters and put up relatively little resistance.

In the sixteen months that followed, the Bush Administration capitalized on its position to make one of the great authoritarian sales jobs in history. It is now common knowledge (though poorly publicized) that Bush and his cohort had planned for the United States to decapitate the Iraqi regime well before September 11th. newly public documents from the National Security Archive show that Bush, Rumsfeld and Cheney had long since decided to invade Iraq, the question was how to justify the action with a plausible *casus belli*. They carefully weighed which arguments would play best with Americans and the world: arms inspections, human rights, threats to Saddam's neighbors – whatever works. Of course, September 11th changed all that, and made "security threats to Americans" the winning argument. Saddam Hussein was no closer to hitting Mars with weapons of mass destruction than he was Cleveland, but it sounded plausible enough to a post-traumatic American mind. Controlled by a handful of ideologues at the top of the government, the Bush Administration began to beat the drums of war for Iraq.

The official news media worked hand in hand with the Bush Administration to make the case to the American people and the world. Lots of serious, gray-haired "military analysts" began making appearances on television to explain the role of "rogue states" such as those in the "axis of evil" – especially Iraq. As the year progressed more and more information about the threat from the nation-state of Iraq spilled out from government officials who claimed to have access to "top secret intelligence" about its renewed capacity to strike the American homeland with "weapons of mass destruction." This gathered steam through the summer, though it crescendoed that fall because, as former corporate executive Andy Card, the President's Chief of Staff noted, "From a marketing perspective, you don't introduce a new product in August." So as predicted, the real theater began in earnest, with many stern-faced interviews from authority figures Dick Cheney and Condoleezza Rice about how Iraq had "connections" with al Qaeda and "may" have "nuclear" "ambitions." No doubt, throughout the halls of Langley, Virginia, in the State Department, or wherever knowledgeable Iraq analysts were seated, there were shocked guffaws of "*how could those dudes have more than a few firecrackers after the military isolation and bombing of the Clinton years*?" Also, "*You mean to say a guy who hates religious extremists as much as Saddam Hussein would arm Al Qaeda? Are you kidding me?*" But the authorities on the TeeVee box had spoken. The Government Has Top Secret Intelligence That Says Saddam Hussein Is Stockpiling Weapons And Plans To Use Them On Us Imminently!

From my personal perspective, I was a strategic analyst working in Washington at the time. My friends and colleagues worked in a variety of organizations around DC, many in a place to know about threats to the homeland. These people came down generally into two camps. One group might shake their head and say, "*Well, Iraq was not high on the threat matrix before September 11th, so I'm just not sure what they are talking about.*" The other group took a decidedly darker tone. "*Are you going to be with us or against us? We're at war.*" I would often expose some skepticism, saying that it was surprising that such an imminent threat wasn't on the radar, say, a few months ago. Then the tone would go authoritarian. "*Look man, you don't have Top Secret clearance. I do. I've seen the intel. This is the right thing to do, and you're ignorant.*" My favorite: "*Dude, I thought you were a Republican.*" The discussion wasn't about whether invading a nation-state with a sixth-rate military 4000 miles from the United States was a reasonable course of action to provide security against non-state terrorist actors. It was about whether you were on the team and whether you believed what authorities told you, when they told you.

The United States, the United Kingdom and Australia went to war March 20, 2003 and stayed at war for the rest of the decade. Hundreds of thousands dead in Iraq. National Guard units pulled from around the country. Thousands of U.S. soldiers killed, tens of thousands wounded, many grievously. Weapons of mass destruction were never discovered.

The six months of active battle predicted by Donald Rumsfeld turned out to be tragically insufficient. But we needed to stay the course. As the inexplicably preeminent foreign affairs columnist Thomas Friedman kept telling America, "six more months." *We know what we're doing here. We'll turn the corner in six more months. Yes, your cousin from the Vermont National Guard is doing his third tour, but we need six more months. We have the intel, you do not. We know what we're doing. We are professionals. We have been doing this a long time. We are authorities on these matters.*

Business management in the decade of trauma

If the story of national security in America in the early days of the millennium was a sad one, the economic situation was no more comforting. GDP growth flatlined in the year 2000, and the uncertainty of the days following September 11th caused chaos in the markets and a drop in demand. Businesses laid off workers left and right, shooting unemployment to nearly 6.0%. American leadership provided no credible narrative as to the future of economic growth, save for the Bush Administration's constant demand for "rebates" straight from the federal treasury and reducing the estate taxes which existed to keep America from turning into a European entity with hereditary land and title. Outside of the odd check for $300 straight from Uncle Sam for no reason, it wasn't clear what our plan for economic revitalization was.

Yet magically, a solution appeared. America had long-since doubled down on its auto-suburb-retail complex, but now it was time to *triple down*. Capital began to sluice from Wall Street banks to all parts of the country, especially to new home construction, home equity loans, conversions from simple ranches to McMansions, condo conversions, and anything else with a six-figure loan that locked the buyer in for twenty to thirty years. *You too could be part of the exciting action!*

You may have asked yourself, as I did, why the hell is the price of real estate going up in an an economy with flat GDP that keeps sending jobs to Asia? Why would the Case-Shiller Price Index double inside of five years when it stayed within 10-20% fluctuations for a century? And the answer that came back, from business magazines to stock analysts to weird new real estate TV programs like "HOUSE FLIPPERZ!" to Alan Greenspan and Ben Bernanke was "*Because that's the way it is now. You don't want to miss out on the action, do you? Because your rent's going up no matter what, sucker.*" It's not like every banker in America could be wrong. It's not like Wall Street banks would loan out forty bucks for every dollar of assets. It's not like they would create a quadrillion in derivatives based on some pseudo-scientific math formula to "manage" all the risk. It's not like Ben Bernanke or Jim Cramer – authorities on these matters! – could be wrong over and over again, is it? Because that would be our entire system of authority collapsing all at once, practically.

This event is close enough that it doesn't require as much historical detail. We're living in the aftermath of this final insult to American expertise. And as for the Obama presidency, which we are to judge at the polls in a few weeks, it can be summed up as a desperate attempt to put the same authority figures back into place. We set Wall Street up as Too Bigger To Fail Banks. We reappointed Noted Experts such as... Larry Summers! back to positions of high economic authority in the White House. Obama SEIZED THE REINS of his incredible mandate to make an economic plan for America's future by appointing fresh new voices to his administration, such as Jeffrey Immelt, the CEO of General Electric who eliminated 34,000 employees in the United States while hiring 36,000 abroad, to head up the jobs council.

Not to worry. They are all authorities on such matters.

Intellectual authorities flourishing in a world of failed expertise

It would be positively idiotic to somehow blame Messieurs Lehrer, Gladwell, Zakaria, Ferguson and others like them for the hot mess of American leadership over the last couple decades. However, their brand of "thought leadership," it must be said, did wonderfully in a world of authority for its own sake. People still needed to feel as if they were talking to *somebody* who knew what was going on, lest they sink into a horrific depression realizing that nearly all sectors of American leadership failed catastrophically all at once. Media properties were looking for towering figures who could stand up across a wide variety of platforms, as billions of dollars of content sales were now concentrated into the hands of a few companies: Disney, Time Warner, News Corp, CBS, and others who owned publishers, TV, radio and more. Speaking agencies had to fill keynote spots for the billions of dollars of conferences held every year, and having superstars is a way easier sale than actually finding the right speaker for each occasion. (*You want to talk international security? Great, here's Thomas Friedman. You want to talk international business competition? Great, here's Thomas Friedman. You want to talk about renewing American potential? Have you heard of Thomas Friedman? He's very influential, you know. Only $50,000, too.*)

If you notice the career arcs of those who attained success against the teeth-gritting backdrop of constant leadership failures, you'll notice that none of these high-minded intellectuals tend to rock the boat too much. Gladwell, for example, has been preeminent in the world of publishing for more than a decade, a period of time covering all of the collapse of character and values I have described above. Can you name a single controversial opinion the man has taken? Has he ever gotten up in the grill of anyone who might hesitate before shelling out his $75,000 speaking fee? I actually think Gladwell is a good writer, but as far as the paragon of intellectual virtue in the Western world for the last decade, shouldn't some part of the last decade's clusterfuck have struck him as worthy of spending a little built-up credibility and inspired him to call some people out on the carpet? I don't mean a Network/Howard Beale *cri-de-coeur*, I mean maybe some minor article recognizing the dramatic drop in results from our leadership, something in tune with the times. Lord knows he could have always regained some ground with a nice book on how people get successful. Fear of starvation was not holding him back.

The defenestration of all these media darlings at once isn't about venal journalists so arrogant that they think they can fake quotes from a Baby Boomer icon in a world of Baby Boomers. The new wave of skepticism is not about a CNN talk show host who is unwilling to admit that most people of his stature have a fawning staff of a dozen go-getters willing to assign their work over to him for a shot at climbing the pyramid themselves one day – if there still is one. Lord knows we're not in a tizzy because some visiting Harvard professor has written a shoddy article about politics in a country of which he is not a citizen. This is about a decade of utter failure, and a culture that is finally starting to ask why leaders all over this country – and the world – are offered as standard bearers of intellectual virtue, paid lavishly, and yet are held to low standards. Only authoritarian regimes create powerful figures and tell you to believe their myths no matter what – ask a Cuban who has been forced to listen to multi-hour lectures from Fidel Castro. Democracies built on the notion of meritocracy, however, are supposed to subject those figures to skepticism and relentless checks and balances. Perhaps, scared and traumatized throughout the decade, we could not bring ourselves to this high standard. I think we are now rediscovering that we can do better – much better. The real question is where we go from here.

America may finally shed its reputation as an adolescent culture

Europeans and Asians are sometimes taken with calling the United States an "adolescent" nation. The metaphor fits. Lacking the wisdom that comes with age, America has tended to create new things with vigor, and also recreate the classic blunders of history. It hadn't had much appreciation for the perspective of its older peers because it hadn't lost innocence yet. Historians many years from now may look upon the early days of the 21st century as the turning point when that began to change. Like the callow youth that gets some experience by living through a few major failures, America no longer has cause to believe in its own invincibility. It has learned that fate can have its way with the country, no matter how bulletproof it felt in younger days. And just as with the adolescent who takes the large, painful step into maturity, it may soon come to realize that things will not be perfect, but life will go on. The two-dimensional myths of youth – in our national case, an unshakeable sense of eternal competence and the belief that bad things only happen to other nations – are being replaced by a more realistic, nuanced view of the world.

As myths change, so shall the men and women who rise to embody them. In recent days, we have picked imperfect vessels to carry outdated beliefs. And we seem to be consigning them to the dustbin of history all at once these days. It is my hope that the next figures to rise will be representative of the needs of the future, not the past. These people could express what we will need to carry us forward – discipline, humility, authenticity, and perspective, among other values suited to a world full of shades of gray.

I can't prove any of this. It's just a story from my point of view. I am no authority figure to whom you should listen because of position, title or mass popularity. Think for yourself as to what all this means. That's the whole point.

THINKING ABOUT THE FUTURE

I have been in the world of strategic intelligence and futures studies since the mid-1990s. I ran my own consulting firm as a futurist for over ten years. In 2012, seeing the dysfunction in how we processed authority, I quit the world of strategic analysis quite publicly in the pages of *The Atlantic*. And yet, I am inexorably drawn to the process of thinking about complexity and projecting current events into scenarios for tomorrow. It's like being in the Mafia; I keep getting pulled right back in like Michael Corleone.

In these essays, I step up with sharp criticisms about how futurists function in organizations. It's something that requires a lot of thought because this is how we decide where to lead our institutions. I'll known the crisis is really over when executives can listen to futurists and other purveyors of foresight without going into psychic breaks and temper tantrums.

GARLAND'S LAW OF FORESIGHT JOURNALISM

Garland's Law of Foresight Journalism is a well-researched theory that guides the actions of magazine and newspaper editors, as well as television producers, regarding their decisions to report on future studies, forecasts, scenarios or predictions of any sort.

The law shows the following phenomena in the media ecosystem:

1. Every publication must produce a feature every eighteen months that either lionizes predictions about the future or attempts to show that foresight is totally impossible, and/or that experts in the field are total fraud. Extra points for doing both at the same time.
2. When the publication in question is writing a piece about forecasting out, say, twenty-five years, it must totally ignore any similar pieces it has written about how stupid and fraudulent forecasting is a scant three years prior.
3. When a journalist chooses sources about either foresight in general or forecasts about specific industries, he or she must choose either the most outrageous proponent of a wacky pet future, or a leader who will simply repeat the conventional wisdom of the industry at that time as if it is an insightful look at what's next.

4. Each article in a publication must be *tabula rasa*, meaning that the journalist writing about future studies must act as if he is the first explorer on the scene at Machu Picchu, and that nobody has ever written about foresight in the past. The journalist must not reference the past fifty years of the field, nor the development of a professional methodology that is applied in thousands of corporations and governments around the world. They should avoid communicating the reality that the vast majority of forecasting and scenario work is not especially sensational, but instead provides reliable return-on-investment by focusing leaders on reasonably certain future trends (aging Boomers, increasing demand for energy in Asia, sales of GPS chips, etc) and discussing in a rational way their implications for the organization.

5. Each piece produced by the major media must underline that the proper way to see the world is in terms of their authority- and celebrity-worshipping, short-term, buzzword-driven twenty-four hour news cycle, and that the only reason to spend time thinking about foresight is to marvel at how exotic and optional it all is. After all, the current intellectual environment created by mass media is leading our institutions to phenomenal success. Why change?

PEAK INTEL

I recently quit my job as a "futurist" and "strategic intelligence analyst" after a successful 15-year career of writing books and consulting to corporations and governments around the world. I spent a decade and a half analyzing disruptive new technologies, predicting the effects of the Internet on the international construction industry, helping executives decide whether to spend billions in the nuclear power market, profiling the customer of the future -- and training thousands of executives to do likewise for their own companies. It was exciting and fulfilling, but this is the end of the road. My employment status is interesting to nobody except my wife and I, but why I am leaving the business of intelligence is important to everybody, because it stems from the endemic corruption of how decisions are made in our most critical institutions.

I am not quitting this industry for lack of passion, as I still believe -- more than ever -- in using good information and sophisticated analytical techniques to decode the future and make decisions. The problem is, the market for intelligence is now largely about providing information that makes decision makers feel better, rather than bringing true insights about risk and opportunity. Our future is now being planned by people who seem to put their emotional comfort ahead of making decisions based on real -- and often uncomfortable --

information. Perhaps one day, the discipline of real intelligence will return triumphantly to the world's executive suites. Until then, high-priced providers of "strategic intelligence" are only making it harder for their clients -- for all of us -- to adapt by shielding them from painful truths.

Many people have not encountered the job title, "intelligence analyst." For the past 50 years, since the rise of the Central Intelligence Agency as a clearing house for information about the Soviet Union, this has been a job that involves researching trends, analyzing their potential impact, and reporting the possibilities to decision-makers. In the age of nuclear weapons, the world was changing too fast for leaders to make decisions based only on their own outdated assumptions. Organizations learned to critically assess their futures -- or literally lead humanity into possible mass extinction. The model mostly worked, and eventually the CIA was joined by other agencies, as well as for-profit consulting companies, which mimicked many of the techniques pioneered in the Cold War. Since the middle part of the 20th century, both corporations and governments have used strategic intelligence, forecasting, scenario planning, and other intelligence tools that keep decision-makers informed and ready to lead their institutions safely through tumultuous periods.

According to the private intelligence industry's view of itself, a phalanx of analysts collect data, assess the risks and opportunities inherent in trends, and provide a series of scenarios that help their clients make contingency plans, such that no matter what future arrives, people will thrive. But the reality of 2012 is quite different. A large number of people promise these services, from generalist mega-consultancies such as Booz Allen, Accenture, and McKinsey, to more boutique providers such as Global Business Network, the Institute for the Future, Frost & Sullivan, and countless individual practitioners. And many executives claim to practice state-of-the-art strategic management, dutifully using the insights of these providers in their day-to-day operations. Still, the culture of intelligence has been in free-fall since the financial crisis of 2008. While people may be pretending to follow intelligence, impostors in both the analyst and executive camps actually follow shallow, fake processes that justify their existing decisions and past investments.

The War Against Foresight

When the intelligence business works, it helps create organizational cultures where empirical evidence and concern for the long-range strategic impact of a decision trump internal politics and short-term expediency. And in the past, many such cultures have thrived in businesses and government agencies alike. But three trends are making this harder, or even leading these intelligence providers to have the opposite effect.

First, the explosion of cheap capital from Wall Street has led major industries to consolidate. Where a sector such as pharmaceuticals or telecommunications (and, of course, banking) might have had dozens of big players a couple of decades ago, now it has closer to five. When I began in the intelligence industry 15 years ago, I did projects for Compaq, Amoco, Wyeth Pharmaceuticals, and Cingular -- all of which have since been rolled into the conglomerates of Hewlett Packard, British Petroleum, Pfizer, and AT&T. There are fewer firms for an intelligence analyst to track, and their behavior has to be understood on totally different terms than when this discipline was created. Where once an automotive industry analyst might have based her predictions on the efficient marketplace theory or classical competitive analysis, now she has to use very different analytical tools. Most of these firms are considered Too Big to Fail by their respective nation-states, as evidenced by General Motors and Chrysler in 2009, and the markets are thus convoluted by subsidies, special regulations, and protectionism. One cannot predict the future of a marketplace by trend analysis alone, because oligopolies do not compete the same way as do firms in free markets.

Second, industry consolidations have created gigantic bureaucracies. Hierarchical organizations have a very different logic than smaller firms. In less consolidated industries, success and failure are largely the result of the decisions you make, so intelligence about the reality of the marketplace is critical. Life is different in gigantic organizations, where success and failure are almost impossible to attribute to individual decisions. Though a given conglomerate might have hundreds or thousands of "executives," each is much more beholden to a complex culture of bosses. Even if people mean well, they're living and dying by a system where the incentives are to seek advancement by pushing responsibility downward and pulling credit upwards. In large, slow-moving bureaucracies, conventional thinking and risk avoidance become paramount, irrespective of how many times a day people at that organization use the word "strategy" or "innovation." It is far more preferable to fail conventionally than to make a daring but uncertain decision without the full backing of the entire organization. Because massive bureaucracies are so much more common than they were even a few years ago, decisions are simply not in vogue right now.

Finally, and most importantly, the world's economy is today driven more by policy makers than at any time in recent history. At the behest of government officials, banks have been shielded from the consequences of their market decisions, and in many cases exempt from prosecution for their potential lawbreaking. Nation-state policy-makers pick the winners in industries, such as automotive, and guarantee the smooth operations of others, such as Verizon and General Electric, both of which received zero-interest cash flow via the TARP program in 2008 and 2009. Eventually, states might do less of directing specific outcomes in the world markets, but for now, these policy-makers have suspended many critical free market principles, and at times the rule of law, on the notion that we are in a crisis, and keeping the system together comes first.

Thus, what use is the old model of competitive analysis if you are looking at markets in Greece right now? Which would have more impact on a given market: the clever, innovative actions of a CEO in Athens, or the politics within the European Central Bank? And how about analyzing the future of the housing market in the United States? Are you going to examine how much people are able to pay for accommodations and the level of housing stocks available in given cities, or shall you look at the desires of central bankers and Congressional policy-makers able to start new financing programs to end up with a desired outcome? How can you use classical competitive analysis to examine the future of markets when the relationships between firms and government agencies are so incestuous and the choices of consumers so severely limited by industrial consolidation?

There is no good way to reliably predict the future in these markets anymore, except maybe by being privy to the desires of an ever-decreasing number of centrally connected power players. Companies still need guidance, but if rational analysis is nearly impossible, is it any wonder that executives are asking for less of it? What they are asking for is something, well, less productive.

The Anti-Intelligence Culture

Strategic intelligence is more and more like reading the Harvard Business Review through a fun house mirror. Sure, people use the words strategy, future, and foresight, but they mean something quite different.

In my experiences, and based on what my colleagues in the field tell me, executives today do not do well when their analysts confront them with challenging, though often relatively benign, predictions. Confusion, anger, and psychological transference are common responses to unwelcome analysis.

While executives pride themselves on being supremely rational technocrats able to calmly assess changes in the world without letting their personal emotions cloud their analysis, the reality is often quite a bit more human. One senior executive shut down a half-day event about future trends within the first ten minutes after a slide warning about "global aging populations" came up. The silver-haired alpha dog not only refused to discuss the fact that their average customer was near the age of social security and getting ready to leave active economic life, he asserted that Baby Boomers are not in fact aging, that "60 is the new 40," that all future strategic problems will be solved by "getting our numbers up," and that nobody in the company was to mention aging populations ever again.

One group of government officials, while discussing the anticipated tax base from housing and retail, became suddenly unhinged when an analyst suggested that those sectors would not immediately re-inflate back to pre-2008 levels. When shown charts illustrating that Americans have ten times as much retail square footage as Europeans, and that housing bubble was, well, a bubble, the politicians angrily retorted that America was special and its population required ten times as many options when shopping. They blustered that houses always regain value and that the multi-trillion dollar bailout was "a one-time mistake."

In early 2009, many European executives were quick to point out to me that the "financial crisis" was a "uniquely American problem" -- and that Portugal and Greece were fine, thank you very much. As European central banks privately rushed to keep the peripheral countries solvent in 2010, I was told not to publicly discuss any such possibilities while working with European groups. They didn't want to hear it.

When a colleague of mine was brought into his employer's "corporate strategy group" a couple of years ago, he saw it as a great honor to be included in the one unit dedicated solely to the company's long-term success. Once allowed in to the secretive confines of the group, he discovered that the mandate of the position had, after 2008, been radically altered. Rather than mapping out how the markets were likely to change and his company might stay ahead, he was made to flip through old spreadsheets to find which products were most profitable, then get salesmen to "sell more of them." When he asked if he should perhaps include analysis of trends in society, technology, and economics to anticipate what long-term options they should be exploring, he was informed, "You need to go back to grad school if you just want to study stuff for no reason."

A 2008 U.S. government report on "Future Trends 2025" made the following predictions: that the U.S. dollar might not be the world's reserve currency forever, Iran would continue to be a rogue nation, China would have more economic power, Russia would be rife with corruption and organized crime, and oil would be replaced by some other magic, stable, powerful, liquid fuel for the world's increasing fleet of cars and trucks. The report cost the U.S. government millions of dollars, all to produce a document that effectively predicted 2006, plus an extra pipe dream forecast of getting out of the world's peak oil predicament, supported by zero technological forecasts from experts in the field. It looked and smelled like strategic forecasting, but was carefully produced to keep from upsetting anyone with scary challenges to their assumptions about the future strategic position of the United

States. This is the new business model for an intelligence industry that once lived to disrupt its customers' thinking, not reassure it.

For too many business and government executives, foresight is a luxury that is hardly necessary in this new "hypercompetitive" post-crisis world. Perhaps it's always been superfluous, we just didn't notice. The study of the future used to be easier to sell, maybe because the analysis usually predicted the growth of the consumer economy or the next great gadget. But the future is no longer nearly as palatable, and the customers are less interested. That's too bad, because companies and governments still need help planning for the future. But it takes discomfort, courage and humility to face that future, and who wants to pay for bad news?

It will not always be this way. When the real pain of our losses and poor decisions finally occurs to people, when the last quantitative easing bailout no longer hides the logical incongruities that are fundamental to the system, and when enough people refuse to believe that "the new normal" is normal at all, we will then return to a real discussion of what is next. In the meantime, the remnants of the strategic intelligence world will be happy to take your money in exchange for telling you that everything is fine.

THE THINGS WE WANT TO BELIEVE

Ten years ago this week one of my best friends was dying from terminal gastric cancer. She was all of twenty-eight. The cancer came out of nowhere, a total blitzkrieg, went metastatic in a few weeks. She was diagnosed in February, gone by June. In May, as the blossoms hit the trees, the call went out to all of our friends to head back to Vermont once last time to see our friend while she was still there.

By the time we got to Vermont, our friend who lay dying was surprisingly perky. The notion of her friends coming to see her was enough to keep her lungs from failing, return her appetite to her, and shock the doctors who had recently given her hours to live. It was about the most miraculous thing any of us had witnessed. We had a famous time, consuming my mother's famous chicken pot pies, gargling cheap red wine, watching bad science-fiction flicks, and laughing.

And then something really strange happened. She started talking about longer-term issues, worrying about where she was going to move next, how she was going to get her credit cards paid off. She was reduced to 90 pounds, hairless, nearly without lung function, but she began sweating her credit cards. Oh, and if any of us had any ridiculous, Shakespearean soliloquy about how its our last time together, you-were-so-special-as-a-friend- can it, she just wasn't interested in the drama of the whole thing.

I was perplexed. On the train up, I was working up big speeches and such. I had had friends die before, but never with this amount of time for soliloquy-writing! She just seemed not to accept the fact of her death. I consulted my aunt, a hospice social worker, who knew these stories forwards and backwards. "She's worrying about her credit cards!" I spluttered. "I mean, it's like she's not dealing with it, she doesn't think it's really happening, even though it is written all over those oxygen tanks she's tied to!"

"Eric, she's twenty-eight years old," my aunt said, "why would she want to believe that she is really dying? What would she gain from believing it? Why would she want to give this tragedy that kind of power by believing it? "

Hearing this idea and digesting it was a turning point for me. My world was surprisingly linear, so I thought. You believed things because of facts, not because of desires. You couldn't change the facts, and you shouldn't change your beliefs just because you don't *want something to be true.*

Then I thought about it more. Indeed, what would be the point of being really "real" about something if that only led to unmanageable pain? Wouldn't a well-constructed fantasy suit someone better than a piercing, horrid reality?

This may be the world's heaviest setup for talking about the frenzy over the Facebook IPO, the final phases of European crisis, the obvious failure of leadership in the industrialized world, but these are the connections I make. Sometimes, the world seems to be completely irrational, and it totally bewilders me, but then I remember the phrase from my aunt, "Why would you want to believe it?"

Facebook as a public company is an absurdity, a total distraction from the real work we have to do on city building, healthcare, education, and other vital economic activities. Moreover, its financial dynamics, 100X valuations and such, look entirely like the bubbles of recent years past, specifically America Online and MySpace – yet the usual suspects are setting people up for a fall yet again. It's another example of real people being taken in by a sweeping scam, a Three Card Monte game that distracts the mark while the guys running the game hoover out their pockets for remaining loose change. People are looking for the "next Apple," but they are just stepping into a very expensive casino, one that is all too practiced at taking the money of the less cynical.

But why would they want to believe that? Wouldn't they want to believe that they are smart, perceptive and shrewd instead? Wouldn't they want to believe that *this time, it's different*? Why would they really want to believe that Wall Street does not offer a positive service, and that they need to pick another investment much closer to home if they want their money to grow without being ripped off?

In Europe right now, people are holding their breath for Frankfurt and Berlin and Paris to make a recovery happen on the old continent. They think that they Euro was and is a fine idea to stitch together incredibly divergent cultures and economies, and that some really smart people can work out the kinks. *Why would they want to believe that it is the end?*

Jamie Dimon has proven that his firm has learned nothing from the debacle of 2008, and for many, his firm was the last one standing that showed any real competence. But surely a trading loss of between two and five billion, probably growing, is a sign that Wall Street may need to be dismantled before the American economy can manage the danger inherent in having such institutions run important functions of our commercial lives. Obviously, the federal government needs to step in and reinstate Glass Steagall, break up banks to smaller sizes, audit the Fed, mark assets to market, send criminals to prison, and set up a comprehensive system of regulations to make sure that Americans can never be held hostage again.

But why would anybody want to believe that? Millions of Baby Boomers are waiting to retire, and they sure as hell don't want to have to go risking their hard-earned savings on local businesses and their own commodity speculations – they want brokers to do it for them. They want their 401(k)s to go up in value, they don't want to rethink everything in American finance. They want their pension funds growing at 8%, no matter what. There is no reason they would want to believe that the financial sector, which was one of the great drivers of American capitalism during our cultural and commercial defeat of Soviet communism, is corrupt beyond repair. It is a sad story.

>>>>

My friend died soon after our magic weekend together. She was peaceful and blessedly untouched by pain. One day she was doing errands with one of my friends, and as they drove by the hospital she said, "Hey pull in here...I am just really tired, you know." And she went in, called her mother, and transcended to infinity. She never became embittered by her bad luck. Perhaps she believed some fantastic things at the end, but that is human, after all.

THE MAGICAL THINKING ABOUT THE STALL OF GLOBAL OIL PRODUCTION

Gregor MacDonald has a new post up about the flattened curve of global oil production, and some interesting psychology behind how people are interpreting it. First, check this trend in oil production, which shows that despite oil prices going up, producers are not cranking up the production to take advantage of the new prices as they have in decades past.

Occam's Razor and Gregor both suggest that the reason that producers aren't pumping more oil is that *they can't*. Because, the desire for profit being what it is and always has been, *if they could they would*.

Today, in 2012, I observe that many analysts of global oil production—and the interaction between oil prices and the global economy—continue to engage in a guessing game about the future. But, frankly, the future has already arrived. And it is not a random future, but a future that was held to be improbable, if not impossible. For each extra barrel of oil produced over the past seven years from Russia, and Canada, there has been a loss of production from the North Sea, from Mexico, from Indonesia and elsewhere. And in the case of OPEC, there has been a stubborn flatlining of production growth, which, in the true spirit of argumentum ad ignorantium, has been taken as proof of OPEC's hidden and secret supply.

Thus, we are led to the newest and strangest meme of all: the failure of global oil production to grow over seven years, in the face of a phase transition in oil prices, is not even suggestive of peak oil. But rather, **proof of oil's imminent supply resurrection.**

You really have to follow Gregor and Chris Nelder and other analysts willing to describe what they're seeing as *peak oil* and check out the comments sections. People with relatively little knowledge about the energy sector becoming viscerally angry when it is suggested that there is a natural limit to consumption. A series of magical assumptions ensue:

- *We'll find an even better energy source!* (Such as...?)
- *We're being constrained by regulation! It's the Democrats!* (Uh, they control supply in Mexico, Indonesia, and Saudi Arabia?)
- *There's actually 10,000 years of oil in the ground, the government just doesn't want us to have it!* (Walmart is having a sale on tinfoil – you should look into it.)
- *So what – we've got biofuels and wind power!* (Yes, and what percentage of global energy supply does that represent compared to global demand, which is rising?)
- *North Dakota has enough natural gas and oil to power us for a century, we just need to invest in its development!* (Please explain how this will fulfill the needs of a national automobile/highway/suburb complex that was constructed when oil was $14 a barrel, and when oil field development was sticking a pipe into Texas and seeing if oil would spurt out.)

- LOOK MISTER EXPERT MAN, YOU THINK YOU KNOW BUT YOU DON'T BECAUSE WE JUST HAVE PLENTY OF OIL EVERYTHING IS FINE GET RID OF OBAMA HE'S A SOCIALISM AND SHUT UP. JUST SHUT UP.

Having seen comments on peak oil articles, I have recognized a pattern. There is an almost religious fervor and blind faith in the denial of what appear to be fairly reasonable, neutral facts:

There's a certain amount of oil in the Earth's crust, and we use a ton of it. It's getting harder and more expensive to exploit. As this gets more expensive, the complexity of our economic system will regress to the simpler, less-energy-intense methods of past centuries – local agriculture, rail travel, etc. We should prepare for this, as it will be vexing.

These conclusions are simple, supported by facts, and uncomfortable.

I suspect that the feeling this engenders is one of *betrayal.* "How could God bear me up into a universe where I'm born swimming in cheap oil, but in my lifetime it goes away? IT'S NOT FAIR. I DON'T HAVE TO BELIEVE IT. YOU CAN'T MAKE ME BELIEVE IT. GOD WOULDN'T MAKE ME RETURN TO LOCAL, SEASONAL AGRICULTURE AND STEAM SHIPS. GOD WOULDN'T TAKE MY SUV AND CONDO AND INTERNATIONAL TRAVEL AND YEAR-ROUND GRAPES FROM ME."

To those of Judeo-Christian faith harboring such latent beliefs, I merely suggest that that you re-read the Old Testament. Yanking cheap oil out from underneath you is the least of God's tricks to those who transgress His rules. And you might notice the pattern in the Old Testament of nations trying desperately to come to a lifestyle which does not invoke God's Wrath. They try desperately to come to terms with how to keep a house, what food to eat, how to run a family, and how to worship. They get it wrong. They get punished, time and time again – floods, locusts, rivers of blood, pillars of salt. And only in the New Testament do they get some relief as to what is expected and how it Works Out All Right in the End.

It has been some time since I believed that our ability to think about the future was uniquely guided by our powers of reason. I believe much more in the hothouse of the human psyche, our dreams, our fears, our spirit nature. But in the end, we must return to reason to avoid calamity. This is one area where the consequences of self-deception will be very harsh. Old Testament harsh.

ECONOMIC DISRUPTION

It is noteworthy that, in the past few years, the economy has been *disrupted*. By this, I mean that after the banks melted down, demand dropped, businesses laid off employees, people are losing their houses, and many people are just plain broke. The shape of this disruption is not similar to the "recessions" we have experienced in the Post War era of constant industrial growth. It is more akin to the end of one system and the birth of another.

In general, it is painful and confusing. People remain caught between participating in the older system that fails to meet their needs, and innovating new ways to exchange value. We are finding our way. It is neither quick nor easy, but we're talking about a major evolution. This story is far from over.

YOUR FUTURE SALES REVENUE IN AMERICA WILL BE GOING INTO STUDENT LOAN PAYMENTS

USA Today notes that America's student debt loan is set to top one trillion, even as the rest of the economy attempts in vain to deleverage. Even more interesting is the fact that the average loan is double what it was just a decade ago. What does this mean exactly?

One decade ago today was October 19, 2001, shortly after the terrorist attacks. We were still reeling from the implosion of the Dot Com bubble. The country was set to embark on a war with no foreseeable victory. Nothing too positive appeared on the horizon. Yet people piled into degree programs, four-year schools and graduate schools at an increased rate. This trend just-so-happened to coincide with the low interest rate policies of the Federal Reserve, making it attractive to banks to lend even more money to young people. And despite the economic doldrums, these university programs continued ratcheting up tuition and fees. This orgy of student debt continued *through* the crash of 2008, and even accelerated after the evisceration of the banking sector. After all, if the economy is bad, you are better off betting your future on additional credentials, no matter what the cost.

Here we are in 2011, a decade into a national fever for high-priced university education, and the U-6 unemployment hovers somewhere around 20% what with unemployment, underemployment, malemployment, and people who have just started dropping out of the system entirely. The nation is one trillion in hock to these speculative educations, and the prospect of gainful employment with a "job" is lower than any time in recent memory.

My guess? The speculative debt educational complex will keep rolling strong, since for many young people it will be easier to borrowing living expenses (food, a roof, car payments) and to keep working on the Masters or PhD than it will be to try to actually employ those pricey talents in the actual economy. But naturally, the future will be affected by these microeconomic decisions.

Remember than unlike other forms of debt, student loans in America are now ineligible for discharge in a bankruptcy. This trillion in debt isn't going anywhere. And the machinery that manages this debt will have no reason to falter. Many private student loans are guaranteed around 4 – 7%, and what bank wouldn't love a return like that? Barring major legislation freeing people from their student loans, this system of debt will be around for decades, siphoning away $100 – $2000 a month from most every educated American who did not come from the top-tier of the socioeconomic ladder.

This should be of major concern to business. Your future customer's disposable income is already being budgeted away by their university. Let us map out the future impact of student loan debt in terms of the goods and services that people could be buying instead.

Sallie Mae has an online student loan repayment calculator which gives us an idea of what the future obligations will be on both subsidized and unsubsidized loans. Let us use federal unsubsidized loans as our guide, bearing in mind that private loans through a bank (say, Citibank) will have less preferential interest rates and payment restructuring plans. Let us also assume a 6% interest rate. The numbers below are from what Sallie Mae calls "standard repayment," the plan which does *not include any reduced payments due to low income*, but consider the impact of this kind of debt if you paid it off without any trickery.

If your total student loan debt is **$25,000**, your monthly payment is **$278**, roughly the price of: **an iPod touch with 8G and some nice headphones.**

If your total student loan debt is **$50,000**, your monthly payment is **$555**, roughly the price of: **a Frigidaire 30″ free-standing gas range.**

If your total student loan debt is **$75,000**, your monthly payment is **$833**, roughly the price of: **the monthly payment on a 2011 BMW 328i.**

If your total student loan debt is **$100,000**, your monthly payment is **$1,100**, roughly the price of: **Chef's tasting menu (with wine pairings!) for two at Eric Ripert's *Le Bernardin* in Manhattan, followed by two tickets to a Broadway show.**

If your total student loan debt is **$200,000**, your monthly payment is**$2,200**, roughly the price of: **the mortgage payment on a home in Saint Louis, Missouri with six bedrooms, three bath, two car garage and an excellent public school system – OR – the rent on a two-**

bedroom in a dodgy neighborhood in Washington DC, (your choice.)

We rarely see the future in terms of opportunity cost – what we might do instead of the course we are locking in. Where the American educational complex is concerned, we are locking out many of the consumer purchases that this waning manufacturing powerful supposedly counts on for economic vitality. And no, this is not the same level of debt that past generations had to take on prior to their entry into economic life.

Is this the future we want?

THE NEXT MONEY: AS THE BIG ECONOMIES FALTER, MICRO-CURRENCIES RISE

People everywhere are fed up with the status quo of the economy. With the passion our official institutions show for this tepid "recovery," many are concluding that progress will come not from the current system, which is after all what got us here in the first place, but from their own ingenuity and inventiveness. In pockets around the world, folks are declaring economic independence by starting small, local, but potentially revolutionary alternative currencies that could change not only how we buy goods and services -- but how we relate to one other in society. If these micro-currencies catch on, we could be witnessing the replacement of our monocultural monetary system, which emphasizes a certain sort of free market capitalism above all else, with a variety of currencies that will represent more diverse sets of values belonging to the groups that hold them.

Local currencies, local economies

The next time you're in the south side of London, you might find yourself standing next to a man purchasing his chicken tikka with pounds sterling that feature, rather than the Queen of England, David Bowie in his Ziggy Stardust era. The man isn't a counterfeiter with a love of 70s glam rock, but a resident of Brixton proudly using the Brixton Pound, a "complementary currency" meant to revitalize the famously tough

London borough by encouraging people to spend their money as close to home as possible. Started in September 2009, the Brixton pound can now be used at 200 local businesses, some of which offer special deals to those who use the currency instead of plain-old pounds sterling. Not that normal British currency is useless: the Brixton pound is pegged directly to its national cousin, and all the notes in circulation are backed by sterling located at a local bank. The scheme is small in scope and totally transparent. And while the paper money is gorgeous and meaningful, it will soon be expanded to allow people to spend their Brixton pounds by text message.

Brixton is one of four "Transition Towns" in the United Kingdom -- the others are Totnes, Lewes, and Stroud -- currently using local currencies. The effort to energize local merchants and inspire local consumers to incorporate their values into their commerce may also be inspiring others.

The Germans are also hip to the local currency concept. Sure, in Frankfurt, where the European Central Bank is headquartered, the elites of the European economic system are furiously trying to stitch together Paris, Athens, Rome, and Madrid in some kind of fiscal Frankenstein. But not every German is keen on the euro. Sometimes to register their protest of this larger system, sometimes to put their economic energy into the prosperity of their lands close to home, and sometimes to express the kind of localized identity that Brixtoners are celebrating with Bowie-emblazoned notes, several regional currency schemes are popping up around the country. One, the Chiemgauer, serves the region Prien am Chiemsee, where it was started by high school teacher Christian Gelleri.

The currency is tied to the value of the euro with some interesting exceptional policies, all aimed at increasing employment in the area, supporting local culture, and making the local food supply more resilient.

In Bavaria, the heart of Germany, many people who once embraced the solidarity of the European system are now turning inward, enthusiastically using the local currency as a protest. The locals are buying a refreshing stein of Hefeweizen, paying in Chiemgauer, complaining about the profligacy of the Greeks, and feeling a profound sense of local pride. Area residents can purchase Chiemgauer notes with their euros, but there are rules for how much it costs and what you can do with it. To maintain an individual bill's validity, the local banks that run the Chiemgauer charge a 2% fee every three months, a way to encourage spending and discourage hoarding or speculation, also known as "demurrage". Non-profits can purchase 100 Chiemgauer at 97€, allowing them to spend 3% of their purchases on their core activities. Businesses that accept Chiemgauer are subject to 5% commission fee should they want to change the local currency back into euros, encouraging them to work within and thus grow the Chiemgauer micro-economy by, for example, getting local suppliers into the system.

Similar currencies have popped up around the world, such as Berkshares in Western Massachusetts, Butte Bucks in Montana, or Calgary Dollars in Alberta, Canada. Like Brixton Pounds, these regional, complementary currencies are tied directly to the national tender, and thus to the health of the overall economy. But this growing trend is also a way for people to buttress local resiliency against the volatility of the global system.

The ancient ways make a comeback

The good old barter system is another hyperlocal medium of exchange to regain ground. While bankers and finance ministers fret about the tangled, abstract mess of the fiscal situation in Athens, the Greek people are living real lives of greater hardship. Unemployment is up, lines of credit are strangled, invoices go unpaid, and retirements are at risk. Yet, the Greek people themselves are still ready to exploit their creativity and hard work for the common good. In the months since the real difficulty set in, some Greeks have begun to meet in the local agora to exchange goods and services directly, an echo of the culture that flourished millennia ago in the very same cities and towns. Since the currency they use is dominated by dysfunction at the highest levels, people are buying and selling through barter. They're trading carpentry for tango lessons, home cooked meals for baby-sitting. The barter network in the city of Volos is one of many that allow local Greeks to achieve a measure of prosperity using their ingenuity and hard work, side-stepping the currency system that is so tied up in unbearable complexities and unsolvable problems at the international level.

The time bank, a slightly more sophisticated version of barter, is appearing in spots around the globe. A central repository keeps track of who offers what services, of how many hours they've contributed to the time bank, and how many hours they're owed. The "hours" accumulate at different rates depending on the skill level required to provide the service. For example, fine carpentry earns more hours than yard work, hours spent doing accounting accumulate at a higher rate than babysitting, etc. Once an individual has earned the hours by working for someone within the network, they can then spend them on the services they choose, with the number of hours remaining being coordinated by a central "time" bank. These systems are in use all over the world, from Chicago to Paris to Moscow, though the organizers are careful to make sure that the time is never given a specific value in a hard currency, which would open the door to taxation from governments.

A group in Northern New England has developed a specialized time bank system that helps people pay for healthcare through their earned hours. TrueNorth, a nonprofit health clinic in coastal Maine, has a deal with Hour Exchange Portland by which physicians accept as payment "time dollars" that their patients accrue through service to their neighbors. The system works well at increasing community engagement and improving doctor-patient relationships, though organizers admit that younger doctors, who often bear hundreds of thousands of U.S. dollars in medical school debt, are less likely to participate.

In some ways, these "new" systems say a lot about the old one. The whole point of currency is to facilitate the barter of goods and services in a marketplace, after all, so it's telling that the buyers and sellers in, for example, Volos felt their government-issue currency required replacement. It's also telling that people would adopt a time bank designed to extract different types of labor from others after contributing their own specialized labor to the economy, compensated through a medium of exchange -- isn't that what money is for? And, typically, our labor is supposed to become currency, which becomes insurance premiums, which becomes health care, so why develop a time-dollars-for-medical-care system that seems so similar? Could it be that the old systems are not functioning quite how they're supposed to?

Techno-money, online economies

Traditionally, money is tied to a locality, printed by a nation-state, and handled either as physical cash or by for-profit financial institutions -- banks -- but that is no longer the hard and fast rule. In the age of the Internet, all you need to "print" a currency is a number of computers tied to the same network and a group of people who want to buy and sell goods and services using an agreed-upon means of exchange. Enter Bitcoin, a currency that is backed by peer-to-peer computing, which engages a network to make sure that the total number and location of "Bitcoins" are managed not by a central clearinghouse, but through a parallel network. BitCoin promises security without monopoly.

The best way to understand BitCoin is to think of it as something like a gold standard. Unless you decorate state capitol domes for a living, nobody really needs gold -- but it is tangible and limited, though you can mine more if you happen to be really motivated. BitCoin is like that, without the rare metal aspect. There are a limited number of "BitCoins" -- fewer than nine million at press time. Like precious metals, each BitCoin can be exchanged directly for goods and services, if you find someone who will take the trade, but it also trades to the U.S. dollar (around $5) and other world currencies.

Why go to the trouble of making a currency backed by peer-to-peer computing? To hear BitCoin Consultancy cofounders Amir Taaki and Donald Norman tell the story, they wanted a monetary system that was secure yet free from the corruption that comes when a few financial institutions have the power to set the prices for transactions. "We were walking around Amsterdam a few years back, and we got a call from a friend in the U.K. who needed a wire transfer quickly for an emergency," Taaki told me over Skype. "We needed to send him 1000 pounds or so, but there were only two ways to send the money, Western Union or Money Gram, both of whom take 20 to 25% out of the transfer in fees, currency spread and what not. We were incensed by the usurious cost of the transaction, but also that there were only two institutions to handle a simple transfer of information -- there was no free market competition at all. We then decided that the hacker community should step up and help this societal problem."

BitCoin is rapidly gaining adoption, now accepted by a variety of companies selling everything from socks to web server space, and is inspiring several startups to trade the currency and consult on how to incorporate it into your business plan. On the dark side, some critics of BitCoin say that the system can be gamed by speculators, or used for such nefarious purposes as drugs or sexual services because the currency is difficult for national governments to track or account for -- though it should be noted that the same is often true for a stack of 20 dollar bills...

An alternative system

None of these systems has become a standard method of buying and selling to replace the existing monetary system. Yet many are finding larger and larger audiences as the crisis that began in 2008 deepens and evolves, allowing more people to do more business outside the "normal" economy.

Heather Schlegel, an organizational futurist for SWIFT, the group that coordinates international transaction standards on behalf of the world's top banks in the world, believes that all of this innovation at the level of local communities is completely logical, and will likely increase in the years to come.

"Obviously, in the wake of 2008, there are flaws to the international monetary system which must be corrected by innovation," Schlegel explained to me. "You have this flawed dichotomy that either the whole system is working great, or the whole system collapses suddenly. In reality, complex systems evolve over time, and new players and behaviors emerge. That's what we're seeing all over the place now."

One facet of the global economic system especially prone to disruption, according to Schlegel, is the somewhat monochromatic set of values we imbue in our currency. "All money transmits the values of the people using it, along with considerable amounts of ancillary information. The U.S. dollar, the yen, and the euro all are 'values' currencies. It's just that the values are primarily in globalization, shallow relationships, high velocity, and free markets. That has a lot of benefits to it, as we saw during the explosive economic growth of the 20th century. It's just that such a currency has a lot of drawbacks, and those are being addressed by these innovations."

Consumers, she suspects, are looking for a way to express more control over their local economies, rather than having the one massive, global economy expressing control over them. "People want fast, free, secure transactions, and the dollar and euro are great at that," she conceded. "But what about supporting local communities or encouraging certain types of agriculture? You need innovation if you want those. That is why we are seeing so many examples of people trying new methods of payment."

Thanks largely to information technology, these systems of payment can be decentralized and democratic rather than tied to big, central institutions. Some innovations are truly spontaneous, based around the needs of communities more than policy makers or investors. Said Schlegel, "The one thing you see with BitCoin or local currencies is that people rarely ask permission from the central organizations. They just start behaving in new ways, and they do so by expressing their values through money."

These micro-currencies aren't meant to knock down the globalized economy, but rather to exist along side it. "This isn't going to be about BitCoin taking the place of dollars or something, or even becoming the standard for digital currencies. As communities begin to realize the possibility of expressing themselves through money, I expect you'll see hundreds of BitCoins, or something similar -- or something we haven't even thought of yet," she said. But unless the world's big economies turn some corner and suddenly becomes quite stable, more of these smaller systems are likely to continue appearing, to meet the needs of communities.

With all this innovation going on, one big question remains: what does this mean for paying the tax man, who wants a single currency to represent all of the activity so he can measure it and take his bite? The national revenue services of the world may need to start innovating themselves if they want to come up with the answer.

THE FUTURE OF JOBS: STABLE POSITIONS, OR SHARED VALUE CREATION?

The use of the term "job creator" is a fascinating political signpost here in America. It is an election year; it is something to talk about, ostensibly to measure up the candidates on their ability to improve the lives of the citizenry. If you remember back to years past, nobody ever used this term. Jobs were natural byproducts of the growing industrial economy. In many ways, jobs created themselves so long as demand increased. I mean, was Eisenhower "a great job creator?" Do we remember John F. Kennedy for his vision of a man on the moon, his steely resolve when facing potential nuclear annihilation during the Cuban Missile Crisis- or do we recall his ability to drum up a few more gigs down at the local pharmacy?

As the 20th Century industrial economy continues its metamorphosis into what comes next, the job is an increasingly scarce creature – so scarce that we want people to tell us about how many they have "created." Funny thing is, people also forget how unusual the job is as a way to integrate into our civilization's commercial life – barely 100 years old. The notion of signing an oath of loyalty to one organization, to plan on decades upon decades of the same type of labor, and of that organization willingly paying for you in your old age – it has more in common with signing up to be the vassal of a particularly well-established feudal lord than it does with participating in a fast-moving economy. Much more common has been piece work and the guild system – I pay you by the day, by the project, when the "work" is done, you move on. You apprentice with someone to get basic skills, or they train you on the job; nobody takes out $200,000 in loans and voluntarily becomes an indentured servant.

Also, it bears repeating, that the very word "job" comes from old English "*gobbe*," or, "*a big, wet, disgusting hunk of something*," a metaphor for a single piece of work, not for lifetime feudalistic employment. And yet, here we are trying to create big, wet disgusting hunks. Funny.

Then again, the mental model of "looking for a job" continues, both on the employer and labor sides. But the dynamic is clearly different than in years past, and this is evident by the assumptions being made by many employers. Clearly, many of them know that "jobs" are harder to come by, which leads them to assume that candidate will accept less than before. Take one "job" I spotted in the local Craigslist. The company is looking for a communications director. Here's what they want:

- Bachelors in communications, Masters preferred
- Minimum seven years experience dealing with major media
- Must be willing to work overtime and travel
- Candidate will be polished enough to be interviewed on behalf of the company

And here's the kicker:

- *Compensation: Contract position, 30 – 38 hours a week*

In other words, no health insurance, and your hourly compensation might fluctuate 20% a week depending on our needs and cash flow. Oh, and if we want to dismiss you without cause, this was a contract, so don't go looking for unemployment benefits.

Hey, all is fair in love and job compensation negotiations. This is every bit the company's right to make such an offer. They are saying to the applicant, "*We want you to act like this is a 20th Century job, be ready to travel, work your butt off when necessary, and even go on TV for us if required. But we're not going to treat you like a 20th Century employee, because we don't have to.*" Obviously they assume the resumés will come flying in, and perhaps they are right. But this kind of deal never would have flown in 1997. People would not have considered this a serious job – certainly nobody with a Master's degree.

This is not a new development in the history between employers and laborers; go back and look up the dynamics of the Robber Baron Age. The assumption was that jobs were scarce and capital owners had all the money. If you wanted a "job" you needed to accept what you could get. This led to major strife, including the birth of the Labor Movement, which tried to reform most of the major abuses in such a power dynamic. But it also led to one such industrialist, Henry Ford, to realize that if you didn't pay people well, then they couldn't buy any stuff. He then vowed to make products of the best quality, at the lower cost, *while paying the highest wages*. Clever guy – he calculated the cost of the Model T to be affordable to his very own workers and made his company one of the most successful in history. (Also the only one not to require a bailout after 2008, for those of you keeping score at home.)

This was one more way Ford was a pioneer. He saw the relationship between management and labor as one that transcended the company, one that could actually cause the whole national economy to flourish. He saw it as more than just jobs, he saw a future of shared value. If we are to thrive, our vision of the future must not be more than creating "wet, disgusting hunks" of something at the lowest possible wage – but in creating a future of shared values through hard work and ingenuity. Not all jobs, it seems, are created equal.

HERE'S WHY WE LET BANKERS GET AWAY WITH IT FOR SO LONG

As the world slowly realizes just how much fraud, double-dealing and criminality lies at the heart of the banking system, there is a slow-motion horror, a reluctance. My God, the LIBOR, to which $370 TRILLION in assets are tied, everything from mortgages to car loans to credit cards – it's gamed from the inside out. As I pointed out yesterday, even The Economist is suggesting that this is the Tobacco Moment, that point at which society gets a hold of the right internal communications inside these organizations and recognizes that many of these firms have gone from opportunistic to just plain evil.

My reaction is: *Well, duh.* Did you see the derivatives scandals? The foreclosure scams? The insultingly high bonus payouts on the very year these firms threatened the world with chaos if they didn't receive trillion-dollar bailouts? Why does it take the LIBOR scandal for us to realize that these guys cannot be trusted, and that a serious new regulatory regime needs to be forced on this industry if we want capitalism to keep functioning?

Answer: *Because Boomers are on the cusp of retirement.*

You don't change horses in the middle of a stream

Almost everybody who participates in the industrial economy believes in saving for retirement. Not everybody does it, for reasons of not having enough money or foresight or self-control, but almost everybody believes in it. Ask the average bus driver, bass player, or Congressman what you *should* be doing for retirement, and they'll say "save money for your old age." Some people are aggressive, and fill their Roth IRA to the brim while hedging in currencies, cash, stocks and bonds; other just have a buncha cash stashed in the ol' mattress. Still others don't save, but know they should. And the institutions you use to hoard this money are invariably: Banks. Preferably big, Wall Street brokerages. AG Edwards, Schwab, TD Ameritrade, that kind of thing.

Well, isn't that the way it's done? Actually, not for everybody – it's a belief system. Ask the Navajo, for example. I got to work with the Washington Semester program at American University, which introduces kids from the American Indian reservations to how things function (ha ha) in DC, so they can take that wisdom (ha ha) back to their tribal communities. The program's chair, Jack Soto, told me all about how natives just can't understand the approach of hoarding cash as opposed to strengthening communities. After all, aren't your children and neighbors and a healthy plot of land your real assets? How can it work out if the plan is for people to hoard while others don't? Won't that just impoverish people? So, there really is more than one philosophy out there.

But here we are in 2012, with millions of Boomers having bought into this game of hoarding cash through financiers. For the vast majority of these people, it's too late to work on another strategy for retirement. That's why *they have wanted to make This Thing work out at any cost.*

The banks are insolvent? Well, prop them back up!

They have trillions in untold toxic derivative swill still on the books? Have the Fed buy it – and suspend mark to market!

We caught the banks seizing homes that don't even belong to them through outrageously corrupt foreclosure practices? Well, just ignore it, I'm sure they didn't mean to do that 43,000 times.

Commodities traders such as MF Global just out and out stole from their customers to pay off their casino bets? Well, heavens, don't indict Jon Corzine – there probably isn't enough evidence to convict him anyhow.

The global effort to look the other way is reaching the point of satire. I believe that the Baby Boomers simply don't have the energy to rewrite the global rules for banking on the eve of their retirement. Dammit, what will happen to their accounts if we actually apply the law and end up scalping the top 175 executives at a financial company? *There will be a run on that bank*, of course. And so everybody moves their money next door. *And of course, they have been up to exactly the same crap*, and so we arrest 200 of their top guys for conspiracy to commit fraud. And there's a run on THAT bank. And so on and so forth.

It should come as no surprise why the world regulators haven't gotten into the gritty business of actually applying the law. It's not where would they start – it's where would they even stop?

But this logic has gone on long enough.

We must get back to the rule of law

If we cannot reestablish some precedent that if you defraud people or steal from them, that you are going to JAIL, then we shouldn't be surprised if the trust horizon folds all the way back to straight barter, skipping these institutions altogether. We need banks and we need credit, but we need trust to make either of them function. As it stands, it has been entirely too profitable to commit egregious, widespread acts of fraud and let the company attorneys work out some non-admission plea deal for a few million to shut the authorities up until next time. Who wouldn't love that kind of game. Who wouldn't keep doing it? The economic benefits – for a few – are probably a hundred-fold the risk. Bankers rarely get investments of that kind of return – so of course the behavior continues.

It is time for new, strict regulations not overseen by industry mavens – i.e., no more appointing former Goldmanites as the foxes to watch the henhouse. And it's time for people to go to jail.

If we don't, then the value of this whole economic system goes slowly down the toilet as trust evaporates. Lines of credit get pulled. Suppliers stop shipping goods. People stop paying their bills. Depression creeps in. And then, it doesn't matter what it says about your retirement on that piece of paper – we're in a future nobody wants.

THE THIRD TURNING OF AMERICA'S NARRATIVE OF GET RICH OR DIE TRYIN'

If anything was significant about 2011 for the United States, it was the arrival of a third major shift in the narrative surrounding success and wealth, courtesy of the Occupy movement.

Post-Columbian America, i.e. the America of Europeans dominating yet-to-be-squandered Indian land, has captured the imaginations of people around the world for more than five centuries, essentially with the same narrative: *you may be poor where you are, but if you come to America, you can get rich from your own merit.* Whether you got off the boat from Vietnam in the 1980s or came to run rum in the 1550s, or headed to the Midwest from Germany in search of thick, arable topsoil in the 1840s, you had the idea that you could get rich. And unlike other lands throughout history, you just might have a shot at getting rich in America through hard work and ingenuity instead of through genetics. From China to France to Sweden to Nigeria, if you ask people what America means, they will tell you a story about getting wealthy from hard work as an individual.

Nobody wants this narrative to change; it is tremendously powerful, and there is little to replace it. There has been so much support for this narrative that even in the face of unprecedented malfeasance and criminality in the banking sector in 2008, the public essentially went along with the plan to make the banks whole, even making them bigger, so long as we don't change the fundamental narrative of America – that *you can get rich if you try*. The trillion-dollar catastrophe should have resulted in hundreds or thousands of white collar criminals going to jail for the massive fraud they perpetrated and for the suffering it caused – but the collective desire to get back to the old story of "get rich or die tryin'" was so strong that we attempted to make the system whole again through no-strings-attached bailouts. And quite logically, those who caused the catastrophe to begin with have quickly returned to the same behaviors that led us to this dark point.

The year 2011 will go down as the moment that this narrative finally began to turn. Perhaps Americans were inspired by the collective, leaderless action taken by millions of people in Africa and the Middle East to throw off the chains of their kleptocratic dictators in Tunisia, Egypt, Libya, and elsewhere. Either way, the Occupy Wall Street meme spontaneously self-generated and quickly spread around the world, raising consciousness about the dysfunction of today's economy. The message from Occupy is on a classic American theme: *Not all versions of wealth are created equal.*

In the Mid-1800s, Americans' consciousness turned toward the notion that wealth created through slavery should not be held as honorably as wealth created through industriousness, innovation, and hard work. The slave-owning states begged to differ, and required total war before relinquishing their worldview. Slavery finally ceased to exist as a legitimate form of wealth.

In the early-1900s, Americans flooding the cities to work in factories came to recognize that wealth created through slave-plantation-like conditions should not be held as honorably as wealth that is shared with those who help create it through hard work. It took decades of struggle, but the labor movement was born, and safe working conditions and dignified wages replaced child labor, grievous workplace injuries, and feudalistic income inequalities.

And today, starting in 2011, America began to wake up to the notion that wealth created through complex, sneaky extraction of other people's value is not the same as creativity and hard work. The Occupy Wall Street movement has popularized the notion of a 1% versus a 99%, those who own the largest chunk of America's wealth, versus those who have the least of it. This framework isn't really to the point, either. America has not suddenly turned away from its narrative of trying to get really wealthy compared to other people, otherwise we would have seen huge protests at Apple stores, professional athletes' houses, or Warren Buffett's place in Omaha.

The narrative that is emerging is that Wall Street provides virtually no value to the average person, while extracting a king's ransom out of the economy as a whole, which it transfers directly to the personal accounts of its executives. Whether from exorbitant fees, high-frequency trading, front-running client trades, or rampant speculation of commodities, the financial sector has perfected the art of taking from other people and adding nothing. This time, we did not have the repugnant enslavement of a single race, or child workers losing arms in machinery to guide our outrage. The perversion of wealth has been much better hidden this time around, couched in tricky macroeconomic voodoo terminology from the Federal Reserve, from slick TV ads for banks that "care" about their customers, and through backdoor legislative corruption engineered by lobbyists. But despite the fervent attempts of the modern public relations apparatus, Americans are anecdotally coming to the conclusion that bankers are still winning and the average person continues to lose ground. From wage stagnation to the cost of healthcare and education, to the steady increase of fuel costs, it is becoming clear that despite having brought the world to the point of disaster, the financial sector continues its pillaging of American wealth at the expense of those seeking the promise of the old narrative through creativity and hard work.

There are those who say that Occupy and the consciousness it has raised is somehow tantamount to communism or "the same rabble we always see." This is nonsense. The fact is, America is getting back to what it is best at – creating wealth through individual effort. Nobody is hoisting chemical firms or construction companies or popular singers on their rhetorical petard. In 2011, Americans began to see the group that is perverting the narrative that has made this country attractive for 500 years. It's the bankers. It is time for their role in society to be returned to its rightful place: at the service of those who create real wealth.

THE EVOLUTION OF THE NATION-STATE

The florid complexity of the global economy has tied together people around the world in unprecedented ways. As a way to increase prosperity and prevent war, we have joined our fates to people most of us will never meet. As a result, the actions of many nations we cannot even find on the map may affect our daily lives, from the availability of rare minerals needed for iPhones in Central Asia to the discovery of petroleum in Brazil.

Something else important is happening through all of this complexity - borders are getting blurry. Our financial systems are woven so tightly that when we go to bail out the US mortgage market, capital is actually sent to France and Germany. American deficits are financed by the global bond market. We hold our breath hoping that Greek profligacy (abetted by American and British financiers) does not collapse the common currency of Europe, thus ruining trade balances, et cetera. We are all in this together, in ways we would never expect.

And then, in the shadows, secession movements are going from the coffee shop to the parliament floor. New currencies are popping up to circumvent transnational systems. The nation-state, an experiment as far as history is concerned, has not finished evolving. I am fascinated by its changes, and have been tracking it closely in the last few years.

THE SECESSION MOVEMENT OF THE FUTURE IS BETWEEN YOUR EARS

The Scottish independence movement got a major shot in the arm from an unlikely source – the elite British magazine The Economist. The clarion of conventional wisdom from London's financial class didn't offer support to Scots looking for national recognition – instead they mocked the whole movement with the cover of their issue for the week of April 14, 2012, entitled "Skintland," British slang for broke.

Ironically, the articles contained within the magazine make a fairly sober analysis of the fate of smaller nations in a world of macroeconomic shocks – but the cover was designed to raise hackles. The cheeky map warns the Scots that their prosperity only comes from their relationship with their dominant southern neighbor, the only thing that separates them from becoming "Edinborrow," "Glasgone," the "Loanlands," and the "HighInterestLands."

Scots nationalists were not amused by the suggestion. Scotland's First Minister Alex Salmon brushed off the criticism with disdain and made a promise for the future: "They shall rue the day they thought they'd have a joke at Scotland's expense." He then points to 2014 as the moment of reckoning for the relationship between the two nations, which is when they have scheduled a referendum on the question of whether to sever ties with the United Kingdom permanently.

The English may laugh up their sleeve, but one person who takes Scottish independence seriously is former Liberal party leader of Canada, Michael Ignatieff, who has personally witnessed the effect of separatism and sovereignty referendums on a national character, specifically those of the province of Quebec. He has gone on the public record to warn politicians everywhere to take the Scots referendum in 2014 as a serious bellwether of things to come. On BBC he said, "The United Kingdom is one of the oldest multinational states in existence. Were it to break up, that would send a message throughout the whole international system. So, everybody is watching Scotland." He points out that even if the referendum on Scottish independence is defeated, as it was so narrowly in Quebec back in 1995, the national character of the U.K. will be permanently altered, as he feels it has been in Canada. Once a serious challenge to national integrity has been made, warns Ignatieff, a people become culturally separate and may ultimately pull their country in vastly different directions.

There are several other movements for political self-determination out there, some ancient and some newly emergent. Given the potential disruption caused by the political machinations described by Mr Ignatieff, we need to ask – is secession a major trend for the future? It seems counterintuitive: We have spent decades building up national and super-national political systems to make us more integrated, not less. Yet as new social technologies emerge, the 20th century economy recedes and transforms into something untested, and people become disenchanted with their institutions from education to money to the nation-state itself – could citizens become interested in smaller, more efficient, more values-driven political associations? And will that necessarily take the form of 20th century "secession" – taking down someone else's flag and putting up a new one, often requiring war or political upheaval? Or will the future of "going it alone" take on a completely new shape?

Why would anyone want a new nation?

Before we head into the future of secession, we should step back in time and understand how nation-states came to be in the last two hundred years, and why discontent is often endemic. All nations are convenient fictions aided and abetted by geography, from ancient Japan to the brand-new nation of South Sudan. Almost every nation is cobbled together from diverse ethnic groups, with the dominant ethnicity taking primacy in the creation of national myths and the exercise of political power. In Norway, where Scandinavian heritage is vastly more common than, say, Lapplander, there is relative harmony; in Iran where only 51% of the population is Persian and the rest Kurdish, Azeri and Pashtun, there is constant instability. As a result, throughout history city-states and regional governments have been more enduring forms of political associations, with nation-states only emerging on the international system in the past two hundred years. Smaller entities have rarely gone willingly into the confines of the nation; usually brute force and repression have been required to make people give up age-old political associations tied to ethnicity and language in favor of the culture of the dominant force in the region. And yes, this is why people have bristled in Barcelona, Eastern Turkey or Western China when you lumped them in with Spaniards,

Turks and Chinese when they are Catalans, Kurds and Uighurs were it not for the stronger armies of their neighbors once upon a time. Everyone's nation is built on a certain degree of this ethnic or cultural quicksand, and occasionally new nations break out, whether it is the peaceful separation of the Czechs and Slovaks, or the brutal birth of the countries that emerged from the former Yugoslavia next door to them.

These days, there are several regions with separatist movements of varying degrees. All national governments are roughly aware of the danger of such movements gaining too much credibility, for they always result in chaos. Today, in addition to the predictable separatists in Scotland, Catalonia, Kurdistan, and the Basque country, there are even more abstract forms of secession brewing. But before these more esoteric versions, let us examine some of the more orthodox examples of secession that might be on the horizon.

Breakaway republics – foreign and domestic

On a personal level, I come from a hotbed of such secessionist activity, one that might surprise the reader. I grew up, like seven previous generations of my family, in Vermont, not so far from the border of Quebec – a place where both of our nations have kept the embers of self-determination glowing for years. While many have heard of Quebec's struggle to achieve sovereignty, Vermont's independent streak will come as a shock to all except a few history buffs. But as many Vermonters will tell you, The Green Mountain State was actually the first republic on the North American continent before it joined the thirteen original colonies. From 1777 until 1791, the Republic of Vermont was closely allied to the new United States, fighting fiercely alongside their American counterparts against the British, even scoring a major victory at Fort Ticonderoga. It even remained independent after the conclusion of the war, but was soon after offered the opportunity to become one of the United States. It accepted the offer on a trial basis, and the state of Vermont joined the Union as part of a 200-year experiment. That "initial" experiment came to an end officially in 1991 – while I was in high school.

This unusual opportunity to leave the confines of the United States was the birth of the Second Vermont Republic movement. Frank Bryan and Bill Mares helped stoke the intellectual fires of secession in 1990 with the publication of a book called OUT! – The Vermont Secessionist's Handbook, which laid out a fun, implausible scenario for a return to independence in which secessionists stun their neighbors by burning bales of the state's famously copious marijuana, pouring maple syrup in the gas tanks of the New York and New Hampshire national guards, blowing up the bridges to the FUS – theFormerly United States – and telling Washington to buzz off for good. The rest of America quickly fell on its knees to beg for Vermont's return, but it had been "one tug on the teat too many," and at the end of the story, Vermont's second republic is reborn. Despite considerable public interest in making this fantasy a reality, you may notice that the American flag continues to have 50 stars – so Vermonters obviously decided to tough it out. But that doesn't mean the idea went away.

I had the opportunity to catch up with Frank Bryan, who teaches political science at the University of Vermont, and who continues to stoke the fires of independence in the land of sharp cheddar cheese and dry wit. He tells me that the best friend Vermont secession ever had currently resides in Texas – George W. Bush.

"People don't realize how much secessionist sentiment was inflamed during the Bush era. The Iraq war and torture scandals really reminded Vermonters exactly what they did not want to be part of in the greater United States. Polls were showing desire to secede getting up between twenty and thirty percent." People came to public meetings through a group called the Vermont Commons to discuss, in the style of direct democracy, their concerns about the direction of the larger nation, as well as to foment some plans for a self-sufficient republic.

But then a terrible event occurred to deflate plans for the reinstitution of the Republic of Vermont: Barack Obama was elected president. According to Bryan, the wind went out of everybody's sails as their hope for change made them less interested in a "free" Vermont. This might have been for the best, commented Bryan. "Honestly, a lot of the renewed interest in the Vermont Republic movement was from a pretty inchoate group. You had people that would show up at meetings who, yes, wanted to form a new political entity out of the reach of George W. Bush, but who were just as apt to gripe about genetically modified organisms in foods or to fret about climate change. It was not all about the political and cultural entity known as Vermont and how it could achieve sustainability on a local level. And that sustainability, that independence is what the people of this state have always been about. Without that, there can be no return to a sovereign republic." And thus, when the swelling and inflammation caused by controversial policies of Bush and Cheney began to recede, so did Vermont's most recent chance at going it alone, content to rely on hunting, logging, and fancy foodstuffs to make its way in the world separate from all the "Flatlanders" in the Formerly United States.

Another state with a long-ago history of independence is Texas. The Lone Star State has a movement called "The Republic of Texas," one that claims that it is not a secession or independence movement. They claim that Texas, following the civil war, never actually ceded its land to the United States, so to retake independence does not require se-cession- it simply requires rejecting the legitimacy of the federal government in Washington, and offering the people a choice. And the Texians (not a typo, this is their adjective) are more organized than their Green Mountain brethren, as they have been steadily forming a shadow government that is rehearsing the basic services of government alongside its United States counterpart. For more information, I spoke with "Republic of Texas, District 8" Senator Robert Wilson who responded to my request for an interview with a representative of the movement. Wilson comes across with the presence of a statesman, being both a professional engineer of fifty years experience and a pastor with a Masters degree in theology and biblical languages. Far beyond any stereotypes you might have left over from the days of the Michigan Militia, our conversation quickly headed for deep philosophical subjects that have concerned everybody from Socrates to Locke, Rousseau and Jefferson.

"Texas was created in 1836 by people who were burning to be really free – free in the way America was promised to be, but ultimately fell victim to the same rulers who made Britain such a miserable place for the common person. Our group aims to recapture those values. As such, the

Republic of Texas does not require secession to pick up its sovereignty. To "se-cede" means to take back something you ceded. At no time did Texians cede their country to the federal government. In 1846 when it joined the Union, it did so expecting the sovereignty that was promised to all the other states. By the time the Civil War began, the federal project was already removing most of the rights expressly guaranteed to those states, one of the reasons we sided with the confederates. And after 1865, when the Union army marched into our land, we were an occupied nation. At no time did we willingly cede our rights, and for us to reclaim those rights, we need do nothing but act like the free people we are."

Wilson is very clear that the Republic of Texas is neither a patriot movement nor a group of protestors in the vein of Occupy Wall Street. The patriot movements, for example, tend to believe that the nation-state is still the right model, it is simply being run poorly and run by people with values that are counter to the true aims of the nation. And protestors are usually demanding a certain behavior from the powers that be. The Republic of Texas has another strategy – the people involved in the movement should simply cease to recognize the rights of far-flung cities to dictate how life should run on the soil that is Texas. As a result, they have no plans to sleep in a park and carry signs, nor do they harbor any visions of "second amendment" solutions in which these problems are solved through some kind of armed conflict. The real solution, according to Wilson, begins between your ears, not out in the street.

"The first question I ask of any person who is thinking about joining – or arguing against – the Texian Republic is, 'Do you know who you are – really?' I don't mean whether you are a plumber or not – I mean, do you know who you are without all the definitions imposed on you by the dominant culture? If you have a sense of yourself, only then can you act like a free man. And if your identity begins and ends with roles you play for other people, jobs you have in a corporation and such – then you're simply not mature enough to see what we are getting at."

Wilson is quick to point out that his philosophy is not radical; in fact, it forms the basis of the Constitution itself as envisioned by the Founding Fathers. The movement, in his mind, is based entirely on common law, the sort of law enshrined in the Magna Carta, not the lawyerly technicalities that make up so much of the federal government.

"We believe that man is endowed with certain inalienable rights from his Creator. Yes, you have heard this before. We still believe in it. We believe that man has rights to control his own destiny on the very soil he stands on, and also the responsibility to solve his own problems. That's why we no longer recognize Washington as a functional entity, and instead are electing our own President, senators, judges, and increasingly, creating the other services of a free nation. And we do not require people who do not even live on our soil to give us permission to do so."

It is hard to say how many people adhere to this philosophy, and whether it will become the dominant system in any of our lifetimes. Moreover – that isn't even the goal, according to Wilson, who believes that the most important thing is to keep this shadow entity alive and functioning, available as an option for those who think of the broader United States as no longer attractive.

"We have sent communications of our intentions to Austin and Washington and we never receive a response. They pretend that we do not exist. They have to. Their worst nightmare is for people to see us as a real option, because they might just prefer the lawful existence we promise to the color-of-law bureaucracy created by Washington lawyers. But we're still here and we're still working on it, because the Republic of Texas never went away – it's a mindset."

Vermont and Texas both have some fascinating undercurrents to their current political systems, but it is difficult to see them raising sovereign flags in the near future. So if America's separatist movements are moribund, what about a couple of perennial breakaway states – Quebec and the Basque country?

The Province of Quebec has evolved its relationship to federal Canada since its incredibly close (49.42% against 50. 58%) referendum on sovereignty back in 1995. It has received a number of sovereign rights as a hedge against further threats to the stability of Canadian national integrity. They received explicit agreement from the other provinces that Quebec is to be treated as a distinct culture, with rights over its own education, culture and legal system. The culture part may seem trivial, but considering the secondary status of the French language prior to the Révolution Tranquille of the 1970s, it was a major point. It also received veto power over the formation of new provinces and other procedural matters of Canadian parliament. While this is not enough to guarantee constitutional stability in Federal Canada forever, it has stopped the threat of outright secession for close to two decades. And while Quebec is currently in the throes of a social upheaval, for once, its people are looking inward and not glaring westward to Ottawa as the source of its woes. Secession seems off the table.

The Basque situation is quite calm compared to recent years, and true secession seems unlikely. Its militant separatist group, ETA, claims to have left the business of bombing Spanish politicians inimical to its goals of a Basque homeland, a terror campaign that cost 800 lives. A prominent political wing of the separatist movement, Batasuna, remains outlawed in Spain, but legal in France. The days of fascist repression of the Basque culture, perpetrated most egregiously under Franco, are gone, and cities such as Bilbao and San Sebastian today enjoy a higher standard of living per capita than any other region of Spain. It is difficult to see a precipitating factor that would enable the Basque country – Euskadi – to achieve separate statehood in the near-term future, though independent sentiment appears to run strong.

On a recent business trip to the region, I was surprised to see that signs in both Spanish and Basque remained unmolested within the city of Bilbao – but that the Spanish words were spray-painted over the moment you left the city limits. And it may seem like a trivial gesture, but watching Basque television, I couldn't help but notice that the weather was reported for "The Basque Country," the limits of which crossed straight over the French border, with nary a mention of either nation-state. The reporter was doing weather forecasts for Euskadi – any associations you might have with EU nations are purely coincidental, of course. Perhaps, like the Texas Republic suggests, the Basques have gone ahead and started ignoring Spain and France in their mindset.

For all the hue and cry, it seems like Scotland may be the greatest hope for the next new seat at the United Nations. The other candidates seem unlikely to be going through the timeworn ritual of forming a new nation-state entity after some period of upheaval, violent or civil. Yet this doesn't mean that political entities will remain stable.

Separatist lesbians and other new nations without flags

If standard issue, 20th century secession movements are passé, then are people happy with the status quo, liable to maintain stability for years to come? Like so much these days, the answer is that not only might we see instability, but it will leverage new social technologies to take on brand new forms.

For more insight on what the next version of sovereignty might look like, I turned to Josh Calder, a futurist with deep expertise in geography, especially the islands of the world. Calder has long been interested in the subject of self-determination, especially since islands are often the choice of site for people who want to secede from the world and start their own societies. He points out that the trend of new nations based on abstract ideas beyond ethnicity and geography has actually been developing for years, if not centuries, as man continually seeks utopian social arrangements. He reminds us that from the Shakers to the Mormons, and to a variety of religious and philosophical subgroups, America has been especially fertile ground for separatists, what with its ample space and immigrant populations already proven to leave the status quo behind.

Looking to the future, Calder points out that nations based on geography and ethnicity may all be formed up, with a few exceptions. However, there still could be a rich and diverse future of sovereignty movements based on ideology.

"Ethnic groups with land of their own can think about creating new borders and becoming nation-states. Cultural and ideological secession often requires a more abstract approach. People can do a kind of virtual secession in which they cut their ties to the society around them. In the 1970s, some American lesbians attempted to do that, creating women-only farms, co-ops, and credit unions, a kind of archipelago of separate spaces scattered across the US."

When somebody mentions "separatist lesbians" as a burgeoning social movement, as a so-called trend professional you have to check these things out. I did, and sure enough, the New Yorker recently did a piece all about the cultural secession movement started by nomadic lesbians living out of vans, a gang whose members all took the last name Van Dyke, and attempted wherever possible to throw off the chains of patriarchy. Sure enough, they roamed in vans from Ontario to Mexico, establishing farms or living off the land, all in an effort to require nothing from the society that tried to ham-fistedly force them into roles as suburban homemakers. This "nation" did not require (nor attempt) flags, diplomats, or currency, but in the way that it consistently pursued separate economic arrangements of barter and subsistence agriculture, it could simply sidestep the strictures of the dominant national culture.

It seems like the bigger trend is not for mimicking and challenging the existing international system, but in simply making the system irrelevant. I have covered two other kinds of secession in a recent piece here at The Atlantic about micro-currencies and their emergence, particularly in places where people are seeking to express their personal values through their economic and political lives.

Transition Towns are places that are attempting to become as sustainable as possible to stave off the eventual effects of climate change and peak oil. Their efforts are surely are out of self-preservation, but an attempt at creating a society with new values is always in the mix.

Local currencies are often part of this transition to new values, encouraging people to secede from monetary systems that encourage hierarchy, hoarding and speculation – not to mention anonymous central control from unelected policy makers.

Bitcoin is another virtual secession in the making. The digital currency, by its very nature, secedes from the ubiquitous nation-state practice of allowing a few oligopolistic firms to borrow from central bank discount windows and charging rents to people who have little or no choice but to become their customers. Being completely separate from the quantitative easing and fractional reserve banking practiced everywhere in the developed world, not to mention its anonymity that is the resistant to taxation, Bitcoin could be seen as a form of secession that fits in your smartphone – no flags or marches of solidarity required.

And while we're on the subject of surreptitious secession, isn't the recent defection of Eduardo Saverin from the America where he found opportunity to the Singapore where he found attractive capital gains taxes just another form of self-determination, this time by a global wealthy elite who are now beginning to claim that the nation-state system is no longer representative of their needs and desires?

The international system is showing signs of either breaking apart or evolving quite rapidly – depending on how alarmed you are at these recent developments. Something quasi-normal, such as people with different heritage and culture demanding their own country, may be something we look back at with nostalgia for easier times.

Why secession and why now?

The renewed interest in secession appears to be yet another manifestation of people growing increasingly disappointed in the institutions that are supposed to represent their interests. Moreover, the more monolithic our systems have become, from megacorporations to regional political unions to currency schemes to tightly woven banking structures, the less change seems possible from within the system. It appears too risky to leaders of bureaucracies to begin the process of evolution, since almost all change will lead us in scary, untested directions. As a result, people are looking for ways to drop out of current practices that won't result in direct conflict with national powers in the ways that tax revolts or popular uprisings will. As the shadow Senator from the Texian Republic reminds us, it's all about mindset.

It behooves all of us to recognize that nation-states are still social agreements, and that as the minds and hearts of people change, so will the political bonds that connect them. As the world changes rapidly in response to economic, cultural, and technological gyrations, so will these institutions that bind them. Instead of homogeneity, reminiscent of the industrial age that defined it, the world will see many different peoples expressing their individuality in a variety of political ways. New nations may be just one of these expressions - and they may not look like what we expect.

THE WEAKENING OF NATIONS

Millions of dollars of Mitt Romney's personal wealth have been recently tied to bank accounts in the Cayman Islands, a Caribbean UK territory with decent SCUBA diving and spectacular don't-ask-don't-tell banking regulations. The Romney campaign protests, weakly yet amusingly, that "the accounts provide no tax advantage to American investors like Romney" but are there purely for the convenience of foreign investors who might wish to invest in Bain Capital without the "entanglements" of the United States tax system. Either way, a portion of Romney's considerable wealth is parked where it isn't subject to the same taxation that the average citizen experiences.

Romney's situation is actually quite typical for a man in his societal position. He has enough money to make himself attractive to a variety of financial odd-duck "nations" around the world who would be more than pleased to "host" his wealth in exchange for the occasional transaction fee, without pestering him about financing their schools, healthcare, roads, war, or any of the annoying trappings of civilization. The question remains -- is that moral? Isn't Mitt Romney a citizen of a particularly large nation-state already? Does he not owe that nation-state taxes, given that he is such prominent citizen that he may actually be elected president of the place? What is going on here?

It seems that the concept of the nation-state itself is becoming a very pliant one for certain actors in society, be they corporations or the very wealthy. The fact is, nations only function because the majority of its citizens believe that their responsibilities to that nation are fixed and immutable, on everything from taxes to dying in war. If we don't make very clear distinctions as to who owes whom what in this world, the relative stability we've come to enjoy in the international system may give way to illegitimacy and, ultimately, chaos.

THE RECIPE FOR A NATION

It's impossible to talk about the ethics of offshore banking without bring up a much broader issue, one that is perhaps overdue for a revisit -- *what is a nation and what does it mean*? The average person takes the concept of a "nation" and assumes that it is concrete. In fact, today's system of states today is scarcely two or three centuries old. Sure, the United States and many other nations are technically older than that, but in reality what existed before was much more fluid and chaotic -- minor kingdoms, duchies, fiefdoms, and principalities, usually squabbling, sometimes cooperating, and only barely organized by ethnicity or language. Historically, states have very rarely agreed upon common currencies. Your identity was instead tied to a locality, scarcely a few hundred miles in any direction, and you probably thought the next kingdom over was the worst place on earth.

Born theoretically with the Treaty of Westphalia in 1648, but not truly coalescing in most places until the 19th or even 20th centuries, the modern concept of the *nation-state* is a larger entity united under a flag -- a very early, pre-Adobe Illustrator attempt at branding. Local dialects were stomped out to make way for a single, standard language. National creation myths were taught in order to give all citizens a similar set of assumptions about who they are, where they come from, and where they are going. All this, plus agreed-upon borders, make up what we now consider an inhabitable "country."

In the 21st Century, every place on Earth is divided into these nation-state things, even where they probably don't quite fit, such as African countries with hundreds of ethnicities and dozens of languages. Regardless of their imperfection, they are the unit of analysis. But that's changing.

ON RIGHTS AND OBLIGATIONS

Throughout the world, we are at a crisis point as to defining the rights and obligations of the members of a nation-state.

From individuals, it is clear: you owe taxes from your income and your purchases; you must obey the laws; if necessary, you must go to war; you can elect political officials so that these obligations are tailored more to your liking. The nation-state pledges in turn to give you access to recourse of grievances and to limit the application of violence and harassment to you from official actors. You get rights *and* responsibilities.

There is, of course, another inhabitant of a nation-state: the corporation. Though originally created specifically as entities that were *not* supposed to receive the benefits of citizenship, in exchange for which they received the ability to walk away from debts, corporations are getting an improving deal as they move through society as actors, gaining the privileges of individuals while taking on fewer of the obligations associated with being located in a single place.

Let us take, as an example, Citibank, the second largest financial institution in the United States. Consider the fact that Citibank received billions in bailout cash. Though publicly traded to anyone, this behemoth enjoys an explicit guarantee from the U.S. government to keep existing no matter what business strategy it might employ. After all, they are an *American* institution, and it is in the best interest of Americans to make sure that it keeps existing, no matter what it might cost in terms of tax money. So when the company got up to its eyeballs in worthless derivatives, the U.S. Federal Reserve Bank sprang into action to make the company whole. Even without the bailouts, Citibank benefits tremendously from the American government, the physical and legal security it provides, all of which is expensive.

What should we make of the fact that the company is owned 25 percent by investment holding companies from Abu Dhabi, Singapore, and Saudi Arabia, none of which governments aided in the bailouts? These foreign corporations get the guarantee of tax revenues that come from welders in Wilkes-Barre, Pennsylvania, film producers in Los Angeles, and school teachers in Manhattan, Kansas, who backstop the risk side of the investment should anything go wrong. But when times are good, the dividends are transferred out to Singapore, Riyadh, and Abu Dhabi.

General Electric has a particularly great deal regarding the nation-state. It avails itself of foreign tax havens when reporting its global income, but then actually prevails upon the U.S. federal government to give it tax credits, recently achieving the impressive feat of having the IRS give them money.

Even our good friends at Google, with their reassuring motto of "Don't Be Evil," find themselves relocating income at will and negotiating with the federal government for the proper times and amounts to recognize taxable returns from its global advertising revenue. You might find this a touch ironic given the fact that Google was established with capital provided by In-Q-Tel, the venture capital arm of the U.S. intelligence community. Quite reasonably, the U.S. government saw a benefit in having a world-beating provider of search algorithms, and put money toward assuring its existence. Curiously, now that said world-beating company is trading at $600 a share or more, its accountants are much more reticent to return the favor of keeping the government in business.

It should be noted that when individuals attempt to place income in foreign bank accounts for these same purposes, they are either arrested for tax evasion or subject to an audit (unless, it seems, they are Mitt Romney caught using offshore tax havens that happen to be perfectly legal). You are probably free of the legal concerns, at least, if you are an individual whose wealth is so significant that it can be arranged into trusts, corporations, funds, and other legal frameworks. In that case, while the benefit to the individual in question might be significant -- qualifying for 0 to 15 percent interest as opposed to 33 to 60 percent, depending on the countries involved -- the responsibility of that individual to pay for offramps and old folks homes is suddenly lifted.

And herein lies our modern predicament. There is a considerable amount of cognitive dissonance involved in all of the political, legal, and financial frameworks we have working in society. The nation-state -- which is still relatively new as far as history is concerned -- tells us as individuals in a very clear voice, "You belong to me, from birth to death. You have rights and responsibilities, and how you go about discharging them will guide whether you get honorific titles and a big house, or a prison cell." And the vast majority of the population of every country has bought into it.

Yet, at the same moment, we have corporations and individuals-rich-enough-to-be-corporations whose money is not fully expected to contribute to any of the projects of the nation-state: security, transportation, health, science. The nation-state whispers to them in a somewhat more tentative voice, "Well, we're willing to negotiate." And as to the rest of us, we're not sure to whom these institutions belong. The nation-state looks the other way as corporate money wends its way from Seychelles to Mauritius to Ireland while lobbyists negotiate special tax rates should the money finally arrive "home" -- but is quick to write checks for all the tax credits it promised. And even a man hoping to be president of a nation-state can look squarely in the camera and suggest to potential voters that he and his family got wealthy from business conducted in a certain place, but want to make sure their friends don't become "entangled" in the system of taxes that is responsible for maintaining the basic infrastructure that made it all possible in the first place.

This lack of clarity could challenge the legitimacy of the institutions we have taken pains to build over the last couple centuries, the ones that keep us comfortable and protected and civilized. The writer Nicole Foss in the blog *Automatic Earth* recently forecast the coming reduction in the "trust horizon," in which individuals believe less and less that these large institutions will support anything positive in their daily lives. All this turmoil from housing bubbles and derivatives and subprimes and currency swaps and Greece and Germany and austerity is eroding the trust we have in top-down institutions. This is particularly true because of the corporations who are first in line to use the nation-state as a wheelbarrow for its risk, and which exploit every rule to claim that technically the income belongs to no one, especially not the nation-state that made their very existence possible, and shouldn't be taxed.

It's also true when you see presidential candidates like Mitt Romney who offshore their own gains from Staples and Domino's and who, should he be elected in November, will be taxing people to pay for the awesome impact of Baby Boomers hitting Medicare, not to mention everything else in the American federal government. We are all unclear on what these nation-states mean, but as the balance between benefit and liability tips toward the latter, people will begin to walk away in ways big and small. This will include tax revolts, already quite common in more corruption-prone societies such as Pakistan or Greece or China, and general flouting of laws, if not revolutions. And as Egypt illustrates painfully today, just because you know something does not work does not mean that you know what to do next.

For those of you who benefit from this mythical being, the nation-state -- including me, you, Google, Mitt Romney, and the government of the Seychelles -- we need some clarity on what is expected from every actor in society, including corporations and the very rich. Enough clarity that you could reasonably explain the world tax system to a ten year-old. The alternative may unfortunately be to get sewing some new flag designs.

THE POLITICAL FEVER SWAMP OF AMERICA

America, land of the free, home of the crazy. This year, I found it impossible not to examine politics with an analyst's eye. Having spent so much time in Washington, I learned that technocrats must stay away from joining one team or another if they want to be able to work in The System. Of course, since I'm not attempting to do that as much any more, I was finally free to say, "DUDE, WTF?"

In the United States, we have entered a period of unreality, myth, cartoon drama, and general lunacy, all voiced by our ridiculous political figures. How could I not finally start making commentary? And it has been fun.

On with the show.

THE BIRTH CONTROL DEBATE IS REALLY ABOUT THE HOUSING MARKET

"But there are no good targets in Afghanistan."

-Donald Rumsfeld, after being told that the 9/11 attacks came from Afghanistan, instead of some place more fun, such as Iraq

America is deep in the throes of its presidential campaign season, never a time noted for its celebration of reasonable proposals, respectful counter-arguments, or civilized exchange between adults. But in the past few weeks, the United States has been the host to a national debate so bizarre you would have thought it was perhaps all a Saturday Night Live skit destined to go viral on YouTube.

Starting with a proposal by the Catholic Church to allow it to remove contraception coverage from the national health plans offered to its employees, the renewed debate over birth control has quickly snowballed into a Battle Royale stretching from Presque Isle, Maine to San Diego. Congress convened a committee, thoughtfully comprised of nothing but old white men. Rick Santorum's main benefactor Foster Friess, actually suggested that women just keep their damn hussy legs shut. And the political equivalent of the boy in your class who farts really loud to get attention, Rush Limbaugh, upped the ante and went on a multi-day rampage calling all women who want birth control giant sluts who need to video themselves having sex and post them all so we can all laugh.

All of this debate is about the housing market. And unemployment. And Afghanistan. And health care for Baby Boomers. And Netflix. And drones. And the bankruptcy of Greece. And more. None of this spontaneously vomited national debate has a thing to do with healthcare or birth control or morals. It has everything to do with a nation that is afraid to discuss its real future, so it would much prefer to re-fight the great debates of the 20th century.

As somebody who discusses the future professionally with leaders of organizations, I will tell you that people everywhere are so terrified of what is coming next that they are fundamentally incapable of having a discussion about it. The American Mindset is almost entirely about Growth and Winning, and the simple fact is that we are likely unable to grow geographically or economically due to fiscal and demographic constraints. Thus, our steady-state economics, or even steadily receding economy, will not look like winning, either on a balance sheet or in people's minds. Americans are addicted to seeing the Dow Jones go up every year. They want their houses to be worth more and more, forever. They want to stay "number one," whatever that means, at all costs. And virtually none of that is likely in the near future. It is so difficult for Americans to consider that they are reverting to all manner of fantastic, irrational thinking to avoid the painful realities that may be ahead.

So, imagine that you are unwilling to discuss the future – but you have lots of meetings scheduled! There are conferences to hold, policies to debate, Presidential elections to run! You are thus going to do all of those things, but you must very carefully avoid any discussion of That Which Is Too Painful to Face. You will then begin having surrogate discussions to channel your passions, because heaven knows, you can neither stop having debates nor discuss what the real issues are.

America is thus falling reflexively into its comfortable old battle lines, the decreasingly valid Left-Right political spectrum. The fact remains, on most issues of The Future the Republicans and Democrats have nearly identical platforms – get this country back to Growth, led largely through banking and housing and financial products, with the goal of delivering the Baby Boom generation safely into retirement. This is so subconsciously ingrained that neither party even knows enough to bring it up. But there is a whole media/political machine designed to create catfights between the two parties, and it's 2012 – an election year! – and thus the Machine must be fueled up and set to tear up ground from coast to coast.

But where to aim the Machine? Like Donald Rumsfeld after 9/11, the Machine is having trouble finding any appropriate targets. Surely we can't bring up the fact that America's healthcare system is going to crumble under the weight of the Boom generation in the next couple decades – what about the healthcare stocks and the lobbyists and AARP? And naturally, we can't bring up the fact that we quintupled the amount of college debt for young people in the span of a decade – young people don't really vote and they don't have enough money to make a big noise politically anyhow. Surely the Left-Right jalopy can't deal with the fact that housing prices will likely be stagnant for the next decade or so, until that back supply of speculated housing is slowly digested after millions more foreclosures. And what of the fact that our military is still stuck in Afghanistan? People don't like talk of defeat or weakness on foreign policy matters come election time. What about the fact that we still appear to have no rule of law when it comes to banking, with everything from systematic foreclosure fraud in the housing markets, to the utterly strange bankruptcy of MF Global, where thousands of farmers lost millions of dollars while the firm was suddenly called a different type of institution at the last minute, and $1.2 billion "disappeared" the same week the CEO was shopping for a castle in the Loire Valley of France. Nothing good to discuss there with the Left-Right Machine either...

And thus we arrive at our collective decision to re-fight the great battles of the 20th Century, a reminder of when Boomers were young and vital and combating The Man effectively. In those debates, lines were drawn clearly between the Progressives and the Conservatives. The only problem is, those battles were won long ago, statues were cast of the generals, and songs written in honor of the fallen. Sorry, but birth control in America is not up for debate – ask any of your bewildered 19 year old daughters and sons. Also, we already settled the issue of whether Blacks and Whites could eat in the same restaurants. Or whether beer should be legal. And whether Vietnam was a good idea. And if colleges could treat men's and women's sports differently. And whether being gay was such a shame that it should never be spoken of. The 20th Century is finished, and its great debates were fought and decided.

And back then they were real debates. The birth control debate *was* legitimate forty years ago. The Pill was a brand new technology that would allow women to engage in sexual relationships without the specter of unplanned pregnancy labeling her a "slut," consigning her to a nunnery or shunning her from the community, as had been done for centuries before. The nation asked itself if this social evolution – and it was a significant one – was worth the public shift in morals to accomplish the greater good of social stability and reduced poverty that comes from planned parenthood. And after much debate, the answer was, "Yes, it is worth it."

Today, there is no such debate. So why is this in the news? Because it is comfortable. Everybody knows their role and they have their lines memorized, practiced diligently during a century of turbulent technological and social upheaval. That's how this thing can play out so quickly and loudly in national media, moving from some policy debates over health plans to screaming that all women are sluts in the space of weeks.

But all of this is psychological transference, the fake discussions of a nation that badly needs to explore its future, and is afraid of the pain that will accompany those new conversations. Until we get the courage to have fresh, important and relevant discourse, I fear we'll be talking about the threat of Communist Cuba and of the danger of saucy rock and roll lyrics for too many years to come.

THE PEOPLE TO BLAME FOR THE DYSFUNCTIONAL HEALTHCARE DEBATE: DOCTORS

America is in the throes of yet another ill-informed, childish debate, this time about how its citizens receive health care. Unless you are living under a rock – which given this heatwave, is a pretty good idea – you know that the Supreme Court of the United States just found that the Affordable Care Act is constitutional. There ironically seems to be more outrage about the Court's decision not to overturn the law than there was when it passed by Congress. One supposes that conservatives, who for thirty years have railed vociferously against "activist judges" who "legislate from the bench," are quite disappointed that SCOTUS couldn't come out *just this once* to rule on political grounds instead of constitutional ones. But of course, the Supreme Court is not there to decide whether a course of action is advisable, merely whether it is "constitutional." Given the wretched real-life consequences of decisions such as *Citizens United*, which invites billionaires, corporations, and unions to dominate political communications, and *Florence v. County of Burlington*, which allows strip searches for anybody under arrest – even false arrests or parking tickets – we should perhaps revisit these expectations for the highest court in the land. And so it is with the Affordable Care Act – according to the Supreme Court, it is constitutionally valid, to say nothing of advisable.

Abandon all hope! America is lost! God'swounds and woe betide us!

The online debate that has followed in a few short days is breathtakingly inane. Opponents of the law went straight into melodramatic hyperdrive, rending their clothes, frothing at the mouth and lamenting that THIS, THIS IS THE FINAL ACT, THE END OF AMERICA! The end of liberty and choice and baseball and apple pie! Everything was going just so great before, and now, here, it's ruined!

The "arguments" in support of this view are frequently comical. There appears to be a strong correlation between being 1) a government employee with guaranteed healthcare paid by the taxpayer and/or 2) being a Medicare recipient and 3) lamenting that government is horrible and too big and thus everybody covered by the ACA is a leech on the system. Never mind whether MY Medicare is funded sufficiently by MY tax burden – *everybody else is the freeloader but me*. America is the land of the free, home of the brave – but not the bastion of the consistent worldview, clearly. Either way, being a vociferous opponent of the ACA requires painting yourself as the last honest man in America, the only one holding down a job or paying taxes, and someone who believes that the only thing threatening the function of American healthcare is "personal responsibility."

Meanwhile, there was similar cluelessness from the cheering camp that said, "YAY! Everything is solved now!" – as if the Baby Boom generation was no longer twice the size of the generation on the hook to pay for this all, as if the economy was not continuing to be cratered, as if the whole mess of a system isn't still on track to be pulverized by the the wildfire epidemic of chronic obesity, diabetes, hypertension, heart disease and Alzheimer's.

Then again, who could think clearly about the Affordable Care Act? The thing is over 2000 pages long, adding yet more complexity to a system already beset by the world's most tangled Rube Goldberg machine of regulatory bodies, for-profit insurance companies, government entitlement programs, tax revenue collectors, hospitals, doctors, employers, and – oh, yeah, almost forgot – patients. It is probably no surprise that America has retreated to its political tribes to yell about the results of this legislation, since there are only a few thousand people at most who understand what is accomplished by the introduction of this law. And perhaps only a few dozen have bothered to think about the future consequences on the health care system, economy, and nation as a whole. Out of 330 million Americans, those are not very good odds for a useful discussion about how to see that Americans are kept healthy.

A lack of clear explanations

Before, during and after the realization of the Affordable Care Act, one thing was missing from the national debate about reform, which careened oh so quickly into the idiot demagoguery of government murder committees and such. That was: a simple list of facts that would explain just what is deteriorating in American public health, why, and what needs to be accomplished. Only then could we proceed into a somewhat rational debate about how to move forward.

The Obama Administration and the Democratic party immediately dove, as is their habit, into bureaucratic language, incomprehensible minutiae, and bland happy talk about what this bloated package of legislation was going to accomplish. And of course, amidst the gargle of tepid Pelosi-speak, you can intuit lots of Good Things that will be the result of the ACA: insurance companies can't refuse to pay for your leukemia care by going back and claiming you made a typo on the application, they can't refuse to cover you because you got a mammogram one time, they can't charge women more for the same coverage because they have complex lady parts; all of that seems like pretty reasonable reform of abuses by a powerful industry.

But in over 2000 pages, there is much, much more than that, making it impossible to really get a sense of what kind of reform we're talking about. This leaves the door wide open for its political opponents to make these histrionic claims that everything was going so swimmingly before, and now *we have ruined this beautiful system by imposing socialism on it, and giving everything to undeserving lazy people, while the hard-working will now be saddled with paying for everybody, which they weren't before – AND THIS IS WHY AMERICA IS RUINED.*

Of course, that point of view is ignorant, self-centered, inaccurate, et cetera. But in the absence of more compelling arguments, we are practically guaranteed to have this kind of lunacy infect the public debate in place of calm, reasonable approaches to keeping America healthy in the years to come.

Doctors have failed in their educational duty to the public

Fingers are being pointed all around in this web of misdirected anger. Republicans point at Obama, Democrats point at the obstructionist Republicans, libertarians point at the Supreme Court, women point at insurance companies, and all are certain of the misdeeds of the other. There is one group who has escaped all mention, and who need to answer for their failings, since they may be the only people who can help us out of this mess: *physicians themselves*. Doctors have failed to come forth and tell the truth about healthcare in America as only they can. They have the experience and authority to lead us to better outcomes, but have been reticent to enter the fray. Beside being terribly busy taking care of wave after wave of increasingly sick, increasingly elderly Americans, doctors are generally opposed to speaking publicly about any matter that touches politics. Their trade groups might put forth an opinion on proposed legislation, but individual doctors almost never do. This cedes the positions of authority to people who almost always have inferior knowledge of the system, not to mention frequent conflicts of interest due to campaign finance – politicians. It may be out of character, but doctors need to step up.

I know from up-close-and-personal how aware doctors are of the American health care system, its triumphs and its failings. My wife is Dr. Katherine Garland, MD FACP, an internal medicine physician and professor of medicine. She currently practices and teaches at a St Mary's Hospital here in Saint Louis, Missouri, a facility which serves a "wide range of patients," doctor slang for "some patients with private health insurance, some with state-sponsored Medicaid and Medicare, and a bunch with no insurance at all." She has also practiced in downtown Baltimore and Washington DC, two more American cities that feature wide swaths of the population that are poor and uninsured. Much has she seen, and so much have we discussed about the day-to-day trials of the convoluted, ill-designed American system of health insurance. Between her and the myriad of physicians serving all kinds of patient panels in America – rich and poor, black, white, and Latino, illegal immigrant and old-line Boston brahmin – a much clearer, much more dire picture of health care comes into view.

Allow me to summarize – no doubt inaccurately – the harsh realities to which the physician community must introduce us, in no particular order.

America already has universal coverage and socialized medicine – it merely has the dumbest possible version of it.

Here is the criminally ignored point in the healthcare debate that every. single. doctor. in. America. knows intimately – everyone in America can get health care when they come to the emergency room, irrespective of insurance coverage. It is illegal for hospitals or doctors to turn away the critically ill or women in active labor under the Emergency Treatment and Active Labor Act of 1986 (signed into law by President *Reagan* incidentally, for those political partisans keeping score at home). If you are dirty, smelly, drunk and without a shed of identification or proof of insurance on you and you walk into an ER and say, "I'm having chest pain" or "I'm having a terrible headache" –

you have just "bought" yourself an inpatient hospital stay and a full panel of diagnostics. Hospitals will receive a $50,000 fine for attempting to dump patients who can't pay. There is a *de facto* system of ***universal coverage*** for the poor, uninsured masses of the United States, it is simply the most expensive possible way of providing it. Doctors should point out that this trope that we're "on the way" to have "socialized medicine" which "would be a disaster" is dead wrong – we do have universal coverage, just a stupid, unfair and expensive version of it.

America's private healthcare system is the world's most expensive by a factor of two and not at all the world's best in terms of health outcomes.

There is a frequent talking point that America has the "best" healthcare system, one that is pure self-congratulatory cheerleading, unsupported by data. It certainly is the number one country in terms of spending, which the OECD lists at $8200 per person, as opposed to places such as the United Kingdom at $3400/person, France at $4000 per person, and Germany at $4300/person. A somewhat controversial study by the World Health Organization back in 2000 listed the United States as actually 37th in the world based on infant mortality, disease survival rate, access to healthcare, and other measures. Some have criticized the report as apples-and-oranges, but still other studies show the U.S. system as lacking on continuity of care and access, not to mention infant mortality (ranking below Cuba, Greece, and Portugal) as well as a variety of other comparators. There is no way to claim we are getting our money's worth.

America's private system is not more efficient than government-run healthcare – it is almost always less efficient, by design.

For all the fretting about government healthcare being a morass of paperwork and bureaucracy, the reality is that the U.S. private health insurance providers intentionally create time-consuming complexity to lock customers into their systems and to create a way to deny coverage based on technicalities. From refusing to pay for hospital stays, to denying coverage for medications clearly listed on their formularies, to inventing reasons to call new sicknesses preexisting conditions, American doctors spend four times as much time – and money on the phone, fax and computer with private payers than their Canadian counterparts do with their national system. Every doctor you know spends hours per day arguing ridiculous claims with mindless bureaucrats, all so they can achieve standard of care or keep their patients from going bankrupt because of denied coverage.

You don't have to go out of the country to experience this either – the Veterans Administration hospital system in the United States, with its universal coverage and unified IT solution for electronic medical records, provides considerably less expensive care, with less growth in cost, and all with a patient population that has more homelessness, alcoholism, drug use, poverty, and post-traumatic stress syndrome than any other hospital system in the country.

This is no coincidence.

Americans are being excluded from the insurance system by the thousands every day.

Want to know the real state of the economy, far away from the stock market fetishists of the Wall Street Journal or CNBC? Ask a doctor. They know that hospital ERs are starting to fill up with well-dressed, sheepish former professionals who have been out of work so long and blown through any funds to pay for COBRA that they have to throw themselves on the mercy of the hospital for cancers that have been waiting too long to be caught in time, for infections that have run out of control, of diabetes that has gone from a problem with blood sugars straight to blindness and leg amputations. Sure, you can look up the statistics that will tell you that the number of Americans covered by employer-paid health insurance dropped from around 70% in the year 2000 to a new low of just 44.6% in 2011. But talk to a doctor, who has to deliver the news that their patient's lymphoma might have been caught early had it been for preventive care – but now society will foot the bill of chemotherapy for a late-stage disease that will also likely kill that person. Get the real story, in all its details, with all the emotional depth that doctors must handle every day in this system.

It is time for a real plan for the future of America's health

America cannot afford hyperbolic, ill-informed partisanship any more. It is clear that America's political leadership is unable to articulate the true state of healthcare with sufficient authority. America's physicians have the most information and the most trustworthiness of any institution left in the United States. It is time to make their voice heard.

The future of a healthcare system negotiated through political gamesmanship is too terrible to contemplate, and a better outcome is possible.

THE THEORY OF OPPOSITES (OR, HOW I LEARNED TO STOP WORRYING AND LOVE AMENDMENT ONE)

The Internet is lit up with hand-wringing about a referendum in North Carolina regarding the passage of a referendum aimed at making gay marriage illegal in the state forever more. On Facebook, Twitter and in the comments sections of all the usual Internet hangouts, well-thinking people are lamenting this step toward a new Dark Ages, a further deepening of injustice, a coarsening of society. After all, North Carolinians voted overwhelmingly for a measure that would limit the definition of marriage to one man and one woman, excluding all other forms, specifically the national drive toward same-sex unions that will open the institution of matrimony to gay and lesbians. Surely, people are saying, this is the end of progress for the friends of equality and human rights as far as people see it today. Woe betide us, and lament!

These activists should take a deep breath, because they are actually seeing the penultimate sign of victory for their stated cause. It may not seem that way at first glance, but the overwhelming referendum in favor of an explicit prohibition of gay marriage is in reality the last step before gay marriage.

I call this the Theory of Opposites. Let me explain.

All over the world we see institutions overstepping in order to defend *turf they have already lost*. People tied to antiquated cultural beliefs are making quite a bit of noise these days. They are marshaling their forces like never before to pass legislation and demand secret government powers and more, all in defense of horses that have left the barn and cats that are out of the bag. Wherever you see the most egregious behavior in defense of something, it is because *the opposite is the megatrend with the most importance.*

This Theory of Opposites is certainly at play here in the gay marriage front. Homosexuality is now widely accepted in most societies, or will be soon in the future – which is why the attacks are intensifying. The fact is, younger generations do not care about homosexuality as a threat to societal stability; their parents may, but the kids do not. Moreover, we live at the point in history when it is likely most pleasant for gay and lesbian people. Centuries ago, open homosexuality would have provoked ostracism or death in most societies. As recently as a few decades ago, homosexuality was subject to regular police harassment, specifically at all-male bars. At the very least, violence toward homosexuals was tolerated in ways it was not toward other populations in society; they were "asking" for it.

Today, we are certainly witnessing a concentration of legislative action in places like North Carolina, where the last set of marriage definition sought to forbid interracial marriage – and California, home of Prop 8, where the descendants of Utah polygamists banded together to make sure people adhere to one lifestyle and set of beliefs, clearly attempting to set a world's record for irony. And with this is a sign the war is almost over.

Glee is on TV, featuring gay high school-age characters, and it produces a minimum of freak-out. *Queer Eye for the Straight Guy* came and went a decade ago. Ellen Degeneres has been out of the closet for nearly two decades. Girls are going to the prom together. For a few hot minutes, the Republican candidate for president had a gay guy running his foreign policy team. Iowa has allowed gay marriage along with South Africa, Mexico and Spain. Look, if corn farmers, the guys who used to have apartheid, and the guys who invented the word *"machismo"* have gotten over guys and girls shacking up with whomever they love, ***the game is over.***

The Theory of Opposites is at play in proliferation of drones and robots for the purpose of "target killings" of "enemies" of the United States and other nation states. All this crazy drone and robot activity appears at first to be the precursor to a scenario in which America will take over the world with a robot army that looks like Johnny 5 from Short Circuit, only viciously murderous. Don't worry – yet. The Theory of Opposites states that the attempt of one country to automate its war-making efforts is not a sign that it will go insane and take over the world, but rather that it really *can't.*

Look – Iraq and Afghanistan may be the last time the United States will put boots on the ground in a conventional war in your lifetime. Sure, the Pentagon "analysts" on Fox News sure play it straight-faced when talking about how great America's wars have gone, and they even rattle a saber or two at the perennial Persian bad guys while they talk about how much "progress" has happened.

Don't be fooled. The U.S. Military's latest foray into Central Asia has been an unfathomably costly disaster. Hundreds of thousands have died. Trillions have been spent, and will be spent in the near future, when you consider the lifetime costs of rebuilding depleted equipment and caring for the thousands of injured for the rest of their lives. Tragically, the United States' reputation as a basically positive force in the world has been torn and tattered. But most importantly, we're running low on oil. The apparent peak of world petroleum supply will be devastating to anybody's intentions for World Domination. Getting tanks up and running, keeping supply chains for men and machines, airplanes, mobile hospitals – it all needs oil, and the Central Asian debacles likely took place in the last decade of ready, cheap, available liquid fuel. General George S. Patton said famously, "*My men can eat their belts, but my tanks need gas.*" That hasn't gotten less true, it's gotten more true.

So why all the dreams of robots and light, unmanned aircraft running around to zap individual bad guys? Because the days of sending hundreds of thousands of teenagers with rifles are over. That oil will be better spent carting our aging populations around and I suspect people in the halls of power around the world know it. Robots and drones are becoming the new faces of force projection, not because of a dystopia on the way – but because it's all we will be able to afford.

SOPA and PIPA were roundly decried on the Internet as the arrival of a new jackbooted regime of info-authoritarians. They even turned off Wikipedia to get attention to this most precarious moment for democracy, ruining the efforts of millions of cut-and-paste school assignments and creating an outpouring of very sternly worded comments on Huffington Post. And the Good Guys won!

The Theory of Opposites tells us that the info-authoritarians are not really that close to winning – and they know it. The ham-fisted legal attempts to let a few companies control parts of the web with minimal oversight was really the sign that our current institutions will not be able to keep control of the power of computers, especially not where antiquated issues of copyright are concerned. The Powers That Be must try to keep their reputation going by giving people the impression that they can still keep a hold of information using copyright – a five hundred year old legal concept designed to keep a monopoly on the printing industry – and using the power of the legal system, which is largely bought off through money and not justice in most countries, and which is completely ill-designed for global issues.

Here's the reality – if you have anything resembling a smart phone, you have a supercomputer in your pocket. The price of memory is still falling; ditto for the price and capability of processing speeds and network bandwidth. Humanity is still rocketing toward a future where every person can keep and exchange every single bit of information ever generated by our race. The institutions we currently employ for a variety of activities – educational, economic, legal, medical and more – are grossly unprepared for the reality this will generate. Are the laughably obsolete companies that control a shocking percentage of the world's intellectual property, both cultural and scientific, attempting to hold on to their societal position with one last grasp before we figure out that the walls are really down? Is it ugly looking? Will chaos result, mass hysteria, dogs and cats living together? Maybe – but I am currently thinking along more positive lines.

So the next time you see a group of aging bigots band together to pass one last flailing constitutional amendment against a group of your friends, take a deep breath. If you see some lobbyist group try to buy your political representative off to pass a law by which they get to control the color blue and the numbers one through six, just shake your head and smile. If it seems like the world is over, maybe you're right, but not in the way that you think. Remember the Theory of Opposites, and the fact that a new era is on the way – much to the chagrin of some who like the illusion of control.

THE LETTER YOU WILL NEVER RECEIVE FROM MITT ROMNEY ABOUT HIS TAXES

Back in January, Mitt Romney was still in the primary race against several members of the Republican Party who were on direct orders from God to become President. It is of course hard work winning against people sent by the creator of the universe to take the job you want, but Romney made it happen. During this time period, it was reported that some of Romney's considerable wealth from Bain Capital resided in curious locales such as the Cayman Islands and Switzerland. As I am quite versed in global business practices of this sort, the use of offshore accounting was not shocking. However, I found it significant that a man running for president of the United States did not feel it necessary to repatriate his money prior to a campaign that would put him under scrutiny. I wrote an article for The Atlantic on this subject about how this shows the weakness of our nation-state institutions when even presidential candidates don't even bother keeping up appearances, attempting to be the figurehead for a country while simultaneously acting as an itinerant financial nomad.

In the months since, the Romneys and their campaign apparatchiks have been playing a somewhat skillful game of cat and mouse, claiming that they have been plenty transparent enough, assuring us that they paid, like, at least 13% or whatever – not that you can check. Snarky articles appear in the media, journalists pepper Romney with questions, but meanwhile the campaign seems resolute in their game plan to remain as opaque as possible.

Let me save everybody some time and spoil how this story comes out. The Romneys are never going to release their tax returns because it will lay bare the structure of their finances, thereby publicizing the tips and tricks used by people in their situation and creating a narrative that will make the "99% versus the 1%" story seem like an episode of Rush Limbaugh by comparison. (*Author's note: Eventually they did release a few returns, showing that much of Romney's wealth was protected by a trust run by the Mormon church, making it opaque once more.)*

Here's the letter from Mitt Romney, explaining everything, that you will never be receiving.

>>>>>

My dear fellow Americans,

I thought I would take a moment away from eating diner food in the flyover states and making triumphant gestures into the air with Paul Ryan to explain the situation surrounding my taxes once and for all.

As you probably know, I am a really, really wealthy guy, which poses some campaign messaging problems compared to the barely-millionaires who normally run for office. Let's put it this way, Dick Cheney was rich when he became Vice President, but I make him look like the hostess at your local Applebee's, limping to work in a rusted out Hyundai with one temporary *donut tire. You see, Cheney was a bureaucrat most of his life, and only got the Big Money Show at Halliburton for a few years between being Secretary of Defense and running George Bush. I did it the right way around, getting stupid rich before entering politics. This way, unlike Clinton and Obama, I won't be forced to give talks at $200,000 to every oil despot and Indonesian financier on God's green earth in order to set my kids up permanently. Ann and I are going to be eyebrows-deep in dressage ponies no matter what happens in November.*

How much money do I really have? Depending on the value of my assets the week you ask, let's just call it a number between $250 million and a billion. Can you really tell the difference between the two numbers in terms of what it means to my place in the social hierarchy? No, you cannot. I don't have a slightly puffy 401(k) that came from making some billable hours and bonuses at some ambulance chasing law firm – I have real money. Bain Capital executed a brand of finance known as the "roll up" strategy, in which we take existing sectors, inject a bunch of money in, buy up or drive out thousands of locally-owned small businesses, kill the category, cut salaries, jack up prices, sell the sucker off, and profit like rock stars. Perhaps you've heard of our exploits – Staples, Domino's, Guitar Center. We rode that final wave of suburbanization and big box retail like Big Kahuna surfers on the North shore of Hawaii. Americans moving out to the Burbs stopped caring about personal relationships with long standing family run enterprises in walkable downtowns, and starting responding primarily to big retail spaces, big brands, and big parking lots near the McMansion they bought with some dogshit subprime negative amortization loan. Our skill was in concentrating capital into businesses that gave Americans what they wanted and little else.

You can't blame us for being excellent at what we did, and I'm not apologizing even if you do.

I was sole shareholder of Bain Capital, which is what led to my aforementioned Serious Wealth. Ann and I aren't your fat and happy Aunt Bev and Uncle Frank, who ran Tuscaloosa's biggest used car dealership for thirty years and now use the seven million they got when they sold out to provide them a monthly income with which they go on cruises featuring shuffleboard and all-you-can-eat buffets. We have equity in the Big Game, the whole system, and quite simply – we have enough money that deciding where to put it all is kind of a problem. Stop snickering and learn something – I'm not kidding, you yokels. When you have north of a quarter billion in assets, are you really going to give it to the asshole 27 year old barely-former frat brothers at Ameriprise Financial to "manage?" Are you going to be one of Goldman Sachs' Muppets, buying the wrong side of their "shitty deal" mortgage-backed securities, or serviced by mouth-breathers so careless they actually manage to destroy all of the equity in your company at once? You don't trust the judgment of people whose real expertise is so dubious that they are forced to run ads during every sports event on Earth until the sun goes out just to keep the suckers coming in the front door. You may notice that Bain Capital never ended up going the way of Bear Stearns, Lehman Brothers, Wachovia, et al. I'm actually GOOD at what I do, so I'll structure the deals myself thank you very much. That's how I got to this level of wealth in the first place.

Now, naturally, when you have money, earn interest, sell equity and make cash on side doing speaking and whatever, there's the little issue of taxation. This may never occur to you, because your relationship to whichever government stands over you is very straightforward – you earn money, they know how much (because you and your employer tell them eventually) and you give them a certain cut of the money, sooner or later. That's not how it works when you have a business, or have enough assets that you yourself are a series of corporate structures more than "a household." I don't make money and immediately prostrate myself on the steps of every single national revenue service where we've done business. There's a thing called "recognizing income." When you're doing billions of dollars of business, it's not like the accounting for your weird neighbor's cottage industry selling Beanie Babies on EBay. It's all a question of the flows of money, the entities involved, how your fiscal year is set up, in which country what took place and so on. You can manage it, and you must, unless you want to pay the maximum allowed instead of, well, something more reasonable.

Do you understand why I'm not excited about turning this over to the American political press? Can you imagine Wolf Blitzer trying to chew his way through this in his stultifying afternoon headline show, much less explaining it to the voters in some swing state?

And yes, there's the issue of the Caymans, Switzerland, and Bermuda. Many people in position set at least some of their assets up in such places for a double benefit. First, it gives you an extra place to store or "recognize" different flows of money, which of course can be quite a bit when you consider the sums with which I typically play. Second, a lot of these countries do not quite report everything that goes down when national revenue services ask – unlike, for example, the pizza joint you work for, which will be dead meat if it gets caught lying to the IRS or revenue Canada or whoever. Some places, like Bermuda, tend not to report anything, making it a little seedy looking, but really quite useful at times.

Are you thinking of setting up your financial life this way? Don't bother. You don't have the money to qualify for this kind of structure, much less the skill to pull it off. This is how people like me manage to get our taxation down to around a third of what you pay. I'm sure it doesn't seem "fair" to you, but, you see, given the laws currently in place, I'm afraid this is just how it works. It's very sophisticated, and I hope you understand why Ann and I have not been relishing putting information of this complexity out there to be misinterpreted, as it surely will.

Now, thanks for listening, and make sure to buy a Romney-Ryan t-shirt before Obama gets his government hands on your Medicare.

With kind regards, hopefully your next POTUS,
Willard Mitt Romney

—-

It's not forthcoming, but it would be fun, right?

LETTER TO A FUTURE REPUBLICAN STRATEGIST REGARDING WHITE PEOPLE

To whom it may concern regarding the United States federal elections of 2014, 2016 and beyond:

Allow me to introduce myself to you, the existing (or aspiring!) strategist for the Republican Party. My name is Eric Arnold Garland and I am a White Man. Boy, am I ever – you need sunglasses just to look at my photo!

If I read the news correctly, I fit a profile that is of extreme importance to the GOP, as I embody the archetype that fits your narrative of Real Americans. Just how much should my profile interest you? Are you sitting down?

- My family lineage goes back to the MAYFLOWER, BOAT ONE!!! (Garland family of New England-> John Adams -> John Alden -> Plymouth colony ->KINGS OF MUTHAF***IN' ENGLAND)
- I am a heterosexual, married to the super Caucasian mother of my two beautiful children who are, inexplicably, EVEN WHITER THAN I AM.
- I am college educated (Master's degree!) and affluent.
- I am a job creator and small businessman.

- We pay a lot of taxes! Every year!
- I grew up in a rural area and despise laziness!
- Having started my own business, I have complained at length about the insanity of federal, state and local bureaucracy – and its deleterious impact on the innovative small businessman.
- I currently live in the suburbs in a historically Red state.

HOLY WHITE PEOPLE, BATMAN!!! *Wow*, you're thinking – *this is not some Mexirican in the Sun Belt we need to attract via harsh anti-Castro policies or appeals to "valores de familia" - this is the BREAD AND BUTTER OF THE GRAND OLD PARTY, a Mayflower-descended small business owner, burdened by taxation, looking out for his beautiful White family in the suburbs of a city (St Louis) surrounded by racial tension and urban blight*!

How can I put this gently? *My wife and I are not sensitive to your messaging, nor did we vote for the candidates you proposed for us this past Tuesday.*

B-b-but, what? Aren't we investors, hard-workin' white folk surrounded by same in a manicured cul-de-sac, scared by a vision of economic collapse amidst the takers in a land of fewer givers? Didn't Mitt Romney's strong family, wealth, leadership history and chiseled chin give us the uncontrollable urge to high-five him into the White House?

No.

May I explain why not, purely for your education, such that you might be interested in winning an election on the national level at some point in the future? It bears pointing out that I should be your Low Hanging Fruit, the easy vote to get as opposed to, say, African-Americans, Latinos, or Asians – and you're not *even* speaking well to me. The reasons why ought to concern you deeply.

As a Card-Carrying White Male I love expressing my opinion irrespective of whether people care to hear it, so let's get started.

>>>>>>

Science - One of the reasons my family is affluent is that my wife and I have a collective ***fifteen years*** of university education between us. I have a Masters degree in Science and Technology Policy, and my wife is a physician who holds degrees in medicine as well as cell and molecular biology. We are really quite unimpressed with Congressional representatives such as Todd Akin and Paul Broun who actually serve on the House science committee and who believe, respectively, that rape does not cause pregnancy and that evolution and astrophysics are lies straight from Satan's butt cheeks. These are, sadly, only two of innumerable assaults that the Republican Party has made against hard science – with nothing to say of logic in general. Please understand the unbearable tension this might create between us and your candidates.

Climate - Within just the past 18 months the following events have come to our attention: a record-breaking drought that sent temperatures over 100 degrees for weeks, killing half the corn in the Midwest and half the TREES on our suburban property – AND – a hurricane that drowned not New Orleans or Tampa or North Carolina but my native state of VERMONT. As an encore, a second hurricane drowned lower Manhattan, New Jersey and Long Island. The shouted views of decrepit mental fossil Senator James Inhofe of Oklahoma that this is a fraud perpetrated on the American people by evil, conspiring climate scientists is belied by such events and is looking irresponsible to even the most skeptical.

Healthcare - My wife and I are quite familiar with America's healthcare system due to our professions, and having lived abroad extensively, also very aware of comparable systems. Your party's insistence on declaring the private U.S. healthcare system "the best in the world" fails nearly every factual measure available to any curious mind. We watch our country piss away 60% more expenditures than the next most expensive system (Switzerland) for health outcomes that rival former Soviet bloc nations. On a personal scale, my wife watches poor WORKING people show up in emergency rooms with fourth-stage cancer because they were unable to afford primary care visits. I have watched countless small businesses unable to attract talented workers because of the outrageous and climbing cost of private insurance. And I watch European and Asian businesses outpace American companies because they can attract that talent without asking people to risk bankruptcy and death. That you think this state of affairs is somehow preferable to "Obamacare," which you compared ludicrously to Trotskyite Russian communism, is a sign of deficient minds unfit to guide health policy in America.

War - Nations do have to go to war sometimes, but that Iraq thing was pretty bad, to put it mildly. Somebody should have been, I dunno –

FIRED for bad performance. Aren't you the party of good corporate managers or something? This topic could get 10,000 words on its own. Let's just leave it at: You guys suck at running wars.

Deficits and debt - Whenever the GOP is out of power, it immediately appeals to the imagination of voters who remember the Lyndon Baines Johnson (!) administration and claim that the Republican alternative is the party of "cutting spending" and "reducing the deficit." The only problem with your claim is that Republican governments throughout my entire 38 year life (Reagan, Bush 41, Bush 43) have failed to cut spending and deficit and debt EVEN ONCE. I hope you understand that your credibility suffers every time you promise one thing for three decades and do the EXACT OPPOSITE. Egads – if you actually were the party of fiscal responsibility – you might win our votes despite your 13th century view of science!

Gay marriage - As the child of Baby Boomers who got divorced (as was the fashion!) in the 80s and 90s, and for whom 50% of my friends had their homes broken by divorce in the critical years before age 18, I sure am unsympathetic to your caterwauling bullshit that "*gays will destroy the sanctity of marriage*." Perhaps if everyone in your generation didn't take the period of 1978 – 1995 to start surreptitiously banging their neighbors and coworkers, only to abandon their kids because "they just weren't happy," I would take your defense of marriage more seriously. The institution of Middle Class suburban marriage was broken by the generation of aging white Baby Boomers who populate what is left of the Republican Party, so your defense is wrongheaded and disingenuous. And moreover, as someone who got called "faggot" about 127 times a day from the years 1985 through 1991 – guess what – I grew up to be pretty good friends with actual homosexuals, whose sexual orientation is usually the least significant thing about them. The Republican perseveration on homosexuals as any sort of threat consigns them to history's trough of intellectual pig dung.

>>>>>>

That's quite enough for one essay, wouldn't you say? Now, given my initial description as a wealthy, hard-working, job creating, heterosexual, married suburban White Male – doesn't your current platform look woefully insufficient to the task of gaining my vote? This doesn't even get into the demographic tensions that show that people of my exact profile are going away permanently in America. You can't even win on what you perceive to be "home field advantage."

Uh oh, wait, I can already hear you through the web browser, dismissing all of my above points because **THAT GUY WAS NEVER GONNA BE A REPUBLICAN ANYHOW, CUZ HE'S A LIBRUL WHO HATES AMERICA AND...**

All right, let's do one last point:

Meanness- Your party is really mean, mocking and demonizing everyone who does not follow you into the pits of hell. You constantly imply – as Mitt Romney did in his "47% speech" – that anybody who disagrees with you does so not by logic or moral conviction, but because they are shiftless, lazy parasites who want "free stuff" from "traditional Americans." Wow, you guys managed to follow up a stunning electoral defeat with insulting the very people you wish to attract for a majority in the political system! Brilliant! You are losing elections because being angry and defensive and just-plain-mean is more important than being smart and winning elections – and thus you deserve everything happening to you.

If you want to know exactly where you failed in 2012, and will continue to fail, here it is. Look you assholes, I'm as traditional an American as it gets, and I do not "want free stuff." I am a taxpayer, and ALWAYS HAVE BEEN. I got my first job – dragging bags of cow manure, horse feed and fertilizer around a farm store – when I was 12. I started my first company when I was 28. I have followed the vast majority of the rules set out for middle class white males (for good and for ill.) And if it weren't bad enough that your policy positions are a complete clusterfuck for the reasons I lay out in great detail, you manage to follow up the whole exercise with insulting me, my wife, and my friends of every stripe who didn't vote for your political party – all of whom are hard-working, taxpaying, job creating, law abiding, great AMERICANS of EVERY COLOR AND CREED.

From this white, Mayflower-descended strategic analyst, allow me to offer you the three strategic options you have before you:

1. You drastically moderate your platform to harmonize with the policy positions I present above

2. You disband the party and reorganize it to reflect current realities

3. You kick and scream and stamp your feet and call me and my friends names – and submit to several decades of one party rule

While I do not want a one-party system, I also don't particularly care which of these options you choose. If you look carefully at the numbers on Tuesday, nobody else cares, either.

Just a word to the wise from one White Man to (presumably) another.

LAND OF THE CARGO CULT, HOME OF THE BRAVE

The 2012 election taught me was that many Americans belong to a *cargo cult*.

Huh? A what?

During World War II in the Southwest Pacific, the Americans and Japanese made first contact with native peoples who had had no contact whatsoever with the industrialized world. These peoples in New Guinea and Micronesia marveled at the otherworldly power of airplanes, radios, clothing and weaponry for the first time. When the war concluded the strange aliens left, taking their "cargo" with them. Man, did the islanders miss all that cool technology and food and clothing! They did not understand why the Gods blessed their people with such a magical experience, only to yank it away so quickly. To attempt to get their blessed "cargo" back, they tried to make things right with their deities, whom they had obviously ticked off. After all, the Gods don't give you great stuff and take it away without some kind of personal failing. *Was it something we said?*

The locals formed religious cults which began practicing rituals to prompt the return of the magical goods. They went as far as constructing "radios" out of palm bark and coconuts to spur the return of airplanes. That's what those guys did to get cargo, right? Then they tried building their own planes out of local materials. Hmm, no good. The medicine men of the tribes also tried to use Christian crosses as magical totems; those must have had something to do with the whole "manufactured goods" thing, right? Those guys were always wearing those cross things; must have had something to do with it. Nail some crosses up and see if we get the magic metal birds full of cargo back!

But alas, the toys were never to return. The arrival of material abundance was incredibly significant to these people, but in the end, they never quite understood what caused it, why it disappeared, or how to get it back.

"My fellow Americans, my opponent is against hangars made from palm leaves!"

If you observed the political debate in the United States this year, ***there were coconut radios everywhere.*** This is a country that knows it just lost something, and it is quite dyspeptic about the matter – but people still can't make out exactly *what* happened. Moreover, the country's current answers for how to get "it" back – or whom to blame for its disappearance – have almost nothing to do with what produced the success in the first place.

Economy slow? People must be lazy!

Pervasive unemployment? There are too many taxes even though tax rates are at record lows!

Erosion of the middle class? Further impoverishment of the working man? Exploding income inequality with the 1% taking 93% of the gains from the "recovery?" People, uh, just need to get a job and stop being jealous! Or something.

Young people not buying cars and houses? It can't be because with saddled them with billions in debt for college – they must just have different values and stuff! Get flipping condos, you hippies!

If America is to form a coherent plan for the future, it needs to separate the difference between the cargo cult and reality. We need to understand what caused America's success, what changed, and how are people are misinterpreting about what to next. Then we can fix things.

First, let's look at the arrival of the shiny metal birds of success.

What was America's great competitive advantage in the 20th century?

In the cargo cult you don't know why you're not receiving goodies anymore – but more importantly, you do not even understand the system that created the goodies in the first place. The islanders could not imagine an airplane factory in Tokyo or California, couldn't fathom liquid fuels and combustion engines, couldn't envision complex supply chains. Today's Americans grew up in a period of historic economic expansion – and cannot fathom just what underpinned that prosperity.

Let's examine the situation in America following World War II. First off, we won, and the Axis powers of Germany and Japan lost. In 1946, America awoke to the realization that:

1. America had ramped up to a historical level of industrial productivity, putting out battleships and bombers and rifles and Jeeps and artillery pieces at an amazing rate.

2. Everybody else who was an economic competitor just blew up their entire infrastructure and killed millions of men in their prime.

America had far and away the world's largest and most intact industrial infrastructure. All it had to do was convert its machine tools from making fighter planes out of aluminum and battleships from to making washing machines out of aluminum and automobiles from steel. And of course, it had a whole generation of young people excited to be alive and get down to the excellent peacetime hobby of makin' babies. This was a boom in the making, in the economic and baby sense.

America was also at a zenith of cultural power – one that would grow rapidly. America had Hollywood and pop music and mass media pouring out onto the rest of the world, the sights and sounds of modernity, prosperity and peace. Moreover, its international reputation was burnished by the fact that it rehabilitated its enemies from the war, breaking the cycle of damaging war reparations and eventual revenge. And especially compared to the spreading disease of totalitarian communism behind the Iron Curtain, America was being made the headquarters of the Free World.

So, to sum up, America had, in contrast to its global competitors who were busy rebuilding their war-torn infrastructure:

- **massive industrial power without rival anywhere on Earth**

- **burgeoning consumer economy, the only of its kind**
- **cultural dominance**
- **high moral standing**
- **rapid scientific and technological advancements**
- **a coming demographic boom (babies)**

Wait, anything else? Oh yeah, HUGE factor:

- **Cheap, easily available petroleum that we produced and refined all on American soil**

These were the strategic factors that gave America a tremendous head start on the rest of the world in the race toward an advanced consumer economy. And in addition to structural advantages, the U.S. government made excellent policy choices:

- significant investment in infrastructure
- massive investment in science and technology
- massive investment in education – GI Bill, student loans, national laboratories, etc

Good stuff, right? These strategic factors plus a general hard-working and innovative characteristic of a diverse people led America to grow economically at a historically unprecedented rate. This is what we refer to as the Good Old Days, scrubbing from memory the Watts Riots, Kent State, most of the 1970s, and our nights at Studio 54. But in terms of goods and services sold, GDP on the rise, and increasing standards of living, this is the America people want to get "back to."

What is causing trouble in paradise?

You never really get to hear about the underpinnings of our economic activity on the news. Forget the availability of potable water in the West, what about shares of Zynga? And forget what the spot price of West Texas Intermediate is today – do you think Kim Kardashian's butt is too big, or does its relative firmness herald a new era of big butts? And how is the Dow Jones doing today?

So let's just update a few of those factors that made America economically dominant to see how things are doing:

- **massive industrial power without rival anywhere on Earth**

The rest of the world has made incredible strides in this area, with several nations rising out of agrarian subsistence economies to become major competitors in heavy machinery, automobiles, aircraft, fine chemicals, and other sectors – Japan, Korea, China, India and Brazil being the most important competitors who have lowered cost and expanded competition. And it goes without saying that America has helped this along by outsourcing so much manufacturing to these countries.

- **burgeoning consumer economy, the only of its kind**

Households spent record amounts supported by: having one income, to two incomes, to two incomes and some credit credit cards, to two incomes, credit cards, and a house we treat like its own line of credit – and now all of the above, plus record indebtedness. America cannot expand its consumer spending any further. It will retrench for the foreseeable future. And now there are millions of Middle Class consumers all over the world to whom one can sell jeans, watches, consumer electronics and champagne. ALSO: we are still recovering from an enormously obvious, stupid housing bubble that has mangled one of the key sectors for all of consumption.

- **demographics boom**

America is no longer receiving a lift from the Boom generation, and in fact as that millions of them turn 65 every year, their spending patterns evolving dramatically toward downsizing and economizing. This is not the driver of economic growth. And their kids are buried under a trillion dollars of student loan debt.

- **cheap, available petroleum**

DING DING DING. America has been a net importer for years. Increasing demand and flattening supply has led to the cost of energy inputs rising slowly but surely for years. **The Good Old Days were built with cheaper and much more stable supply of petroleum. The implications of this cannot be overstated.**

Quick question: how often do you see strategic issues like this in the national dialogue – especially the political dialogue we just had for what felt like an interminable period?

Strategic thinking in the cargo cult

One of the persistent themes of the election that we just had in the United States was *just how wrong things feel.* Especially where the presidential election was concerned, this was expressed over and over. If you were in Obama camp, perhaps you know that things are not good in

America, and surely we must stay the current course, that recovery is happening *but you just can't feel it*, as Bill Clinton (one of America's best feelers) said at the Democratic National Convention.

If you were a Republican, the theme was usually apocalyptic, that Obama's policies were the sole reason behind this malaise – and that things are getting worse because of his policies. That and he's a Marxist Kenyan Anti-Colonialist Elitist Black Power Islamist Satanist. So HE IS AT FAULT FOR EVERYTHING!!!!

Collectively, we got the following potential strategies from our leaders this past campaign season from Democrats:

- Do the same stuff, more competently.
- Expand some regulations to incrementally alter the playing field.

From the Republicans we got:

- Privatize social security
- Shut down Planned Parenthood!
- Cut taxes on the wealthy!
- Overturn that horrible Obamacare thingee which is like Russian Communism, but worse!!!!11
- Stop the march of the Marxists, that's what!

QUESTION: How much of what we just heard has a lick to do with our real problems? How much of what we just heard was an actual discussion about the state of the nation? How much of this has to do with the real source of America's past success, and how much was just a bunch of coconut radios?

Did we talk about the effect of the millions of Baby Boomers hitting retirement age?

Did anybody come clean on how much health insurance is going to explode with or without Obamacare?

Are we planning to deal with rising and erratic oil prices by building public transit, changing city design, or mandating fuel efficiency?

Are we bringing any of those manufacturing jobs back?

Is the price of college supposed to just go up forever?

Will we get around to upgrading America's crumbling bridges, railways, and electrical grid?

Are we living in the real world, or are we running around making a cargo cult, angry that the Gods haven't given us our toys back, but unable to perceive what would actually restore the nation?

The islanders did the best with what they had – zero experience of modern industrial society and a mentality suited to Stone Age living.

We should know better. Generations before us understood what made lasting prosperity. And we're choosing a cargo cult on purpose.

ON AMERICAN CULTURE LEAVING ITS ADOLESCENCE

If there is so much to discuss about America's approach to politics, I suspect it is because the country itself is undergoing a major transformation. There is the aforementioned economic disruption, turning away from the automobile-based housing and retail bubble. There are, I believe, deeper psychological elements at play. We Americans have had to deal with the realization that we too can be hurt (9/11) and that perhaps our business prowess is not without its limits (the crash of 2008.) We are, in many ways, growing up. The process of maturing can be witnessed from a number of angles, including through the Footloose remake, and college football. America is a strange and fascinating country. Stay tuned.

THE FOOTLOOSE REMAKE IS WHY WE ARE IN A DEPRESSION

I want you to consider the psycho-econo-cultural impact of the remake of Footloose, which, in contravention of all remaining humanity, opens tonight.

Mein Gott in Himmel, has it really come to this in American culture? What exactly was left unanswered about that most sweeping, timeless narrative in the way it was portrayed by Kevin Bacon? In which dark, psychotic corner of this nation is there a social movement constraining the music of Kenny Loggins as the enemy of public decency? Every kid in America can watch *Dancing with the Stars* and *So You Think You Can Dance* – how exactly would dancing be rebellion? What are kids going to make of the verbal fencing around the word "pansy" when kids are openly going to the prom with same-sex partners, and gay marriage is a legal option is several states? What purpose could this pseudo-artistic scar tissue possibly serve on this beautiful and holy Earth?

What? They are remaking Dirty Dancing, too? AT LONG LAST SIR, HAVE YOU NO DECENCY -p8t756i edjrtdf ghjd bhcgfgcdsiu ydosy7y*%@(!*&(*&&(@&*#

Pardon me.

This repetitive gobbledygook is why the world economy is continuing to collapse and why your kid is still living in your basement despite having earned three college degrees. It isn't a symptom, it is the cause. Seriously.

The executive decisions that lead to remakes of essentially perfect films like Footloose and Dirty Dancing are purely the result of a bunker mentality, fear of the most primeval sort. The fundamental logic of the modern conglomerate is constant growth at any cost. This growth is no longer possible for demographic, financial and technological reasons. There are still billions of people looking to be entertained, but the way this needs to happen will run counter to the endless growth of the current media business model. So the executives involved would rather greenlight something like Dirty Dancing, with guaranteed revenue due to name recognition, than to take a chance and allow something new to emerge. Endless growth at all costs does not tolerate failure, nor innovation, nor risk, nor growth, nor humanity. Endless growth would rather fail at attempting what produced growth in the past than to attempt something with a future and risk even a flat return.

We are doing this everywhere, and the results are predictably perverse.

We are choking on debt at both the personal and national level...so we pump up the money supply so "businesses can get lending again" and governments can run even bigger deficits.

Our banks were so large and conglomerated that they threatened to destroy the world economy...so we made them even bigger.

The car-suburb-retail complex has destroyed many of our cities, annihilated small retail and left us dependent on oil that is at peak global supply...so we bail out car companies, dump money into "shovel-ready" roads projects, and shortchange the railways and trolleys which will actually enable the next economy.

We lost sight of what real prosperity looks like in favor of Dot Com illusions, flipped houses and bogus financial instruments...so Boomers continue to obsess about the Dow Jones and their nominal investments as a way to assure a dignified retirement.

What used to provide growth and vitality no longer works...so we do more of it. It is the only sure way to get back to some mythical time when everything was perfect.

We are witnessing the death of emergence. There was a time when new ideas, products, companies, bands, fashion trends and movies emerged on the scene, capturing the public's imagination and driving economic vitality. When these things emerged, they made people look forward, not back. And they were never sure things. *Star Wars*, one of the biggest films in history, was passed by most of the studios, and most of the films' actors thought it would be an embarrassing flop until it set the world on fire. *Dirty Dancing* was a fluke, a $6 million picture that starred this minor actor whose Mom happened to run a dance studio and who looked pretty good doing the rumba. *Microsoft*, for that matter, was the second-choice vendor for the operating system of the PC, not a done deal by any stretch of the imagination. *Things emerge* to take advantage of people's imaginations as a result of somebody taking a risk, with the potential of failure looming ever present.

There's a kid out there with a vision for a film, a book, a company, a medical technology. These things will illuminate us, solve our problems, make us dream, improve our health...so long as they are able to emerge. As long as someone takes a risk. So long as the money and man-hours are not tied up trying to rerelease a movie from the 1980s just to desperately cling to the notion of a sure thing.

When we regain that ability, this Depression will lift, and we will move forward.

JOE PATERNO AND A CULTURE DRIVEN TO DISTRACTION

America is trying to wrap its head around the Freeh Report that shows the perversion at every level of Jerry Sandusky's rampage of child rape that lasted more than a decade. A jury has already convicted Sandusky of the crimes themselves. It took former FBI director Louis Freeh to uncover, through an analysis of 3.5 million emails dating back fourteen years, that the senior athletic and administrative staff enabled the entire sick affair. A posthumous letter from coach Joe Paterno himself attempts to cast attention away from his beloved football program claiming that "this is not a football scandal." And he is right – the Sandusky-Paterno affair is far bigger than any one sport. It exposes a deep dysfunction in a nation that has tragically confused its frivolous entertainments for things that are practically and morally important to our real lives. Our collective future depends on our ability to grow up and focus on the many challenges before this society.

The supreme power of entertainment in American culture

One thing you hear around Penn State football is that it was a religion and Joe Paterno one of its high priests. People speak about the incredible power that the man wielded in the state of Pennsylvania. A number of observers have claimed that Paterno was the most important person at the university. Certainly, many witnesses in the Sandusky prosecution claimed to be afraid to come forward to confront a cadre of men who led the single most important activity at their place of employment for fear of losing their jobs – or worse. The janitors were no better than the senior administrators, who to this day fear retribution from the same mob of supporters who rioted upon the coach's termination. Any way you slice it, Joe Paterno was the individual with the most raw power in the university, if not the area, if not the state.

And for what activity did he achieve this power? *For coaching men who play a game with a ball.* Paterno was not the head of the army or a financier or the state's largest employer or an elected official – his organization ran around some grass with a ball versus other men who did likewise. He achieved supreme power in an activity that is virtually without importance.

For every sports superfan currently hyperventilating and letting out streams of profanity along with numb explanations of the "commitment to excellence, community involvement, important-to-millions" argument – you are proving my point. Sports are fun. Sports are popular. Sports make a lot of money. You like them. I like them. But that does not make them important activities, and the fact that our culture has lost sight of this is precisely why Jerry Sandusky was allowed to use Penn State football facilities as his personal torture chamber. People all around the program believed in their hearts that protecting a college football team from embarrassment was so important that it even superseded going to the police over rapes that were witnessed on campus. The Freeh Report shows without question that the people involved believed that this activity actually took precedence over child welfare.

Our most important value is making money

The real problem is that the executives at Penn State are not the only people who would have made this decision. Many cities, regions and states have their own cults of personality that form around sports, cults that downplay illegal, unethical and immoral acts. Look at the rehabilitation of Michael Vick, a man in the sports entertainment industry convicted of torturing animals. One would think that an industry that markets to children would be loathe to place a man convicted of such grotesque brutality back in the spotlight – but the argument was that he was talented and a moneymaker. His prowess and profitability, at the end of the day, came before any of the high-minded values of character and excellence we see trotted out so often in regards to sports. And if you want further examples of illegality glossed over by performance, read the documents pertaining to Kobe Bryant's rape case – settled out of court for an undisclosed sum – and then look at the improvement to his reputation after athletic feats such as his subsequent 81-point game versus the Toronto Raptors. At the end of the day, that which is supposed to be a fun diversion, an elevation of positive characteristics, is in actuality a calculated business arrangement with its own logic that trumps morality. Whether we intend it or not, these are the lessons we are passing on to our children as they build the next generation of our civilization – that *anything is forgivable as long as you make money*. Unfortunately, that lesson, intended or not, goes on to inform behaviors in every other institution of society.

It is time to put childish things back in their place

This is what Paterno and Sandusky should remind us – *it's only a game*. The fact that men put a game ahead of child safety is the warning of all warnings about the culture's insatiable need to be entertained. It reminds me of the fervor on Wall Street over companies that produce no other product other than distraction. We hear about Zynga, makers of FarmVille, or Angry Birds or even Facebook, all of which are distractions that can guarantee "eyeballs" in the parlance of marketers. We're more interested in FarmVille than farming, more interested in Instagram than manufacturing, more involved with Facebook's IPO than we are the unprecedented unemployment for college graduates in America.

And none of these things are important – not sports, not games, not movies. It is a testament to the phenomenal economic success of the United States that we could forget what is truly important, where prior generations had to claw the dirt with their own fingernails just to make a living. We have been so successful as to ignore healthcare, city planning, taking care of elders, and energy efficiency in favor of distractions. The Penn State affair shows us just how far afield our mentality has strayed.

In the Bible, 1 Corinthians 13:11 states that "*when I was a child, I spoke like a child, reasoned like a child – but when the time came I put away childish things.*" America is entering a phase of its existence where the tolerance for childish things shall be reduced by the new challenges we will face from demographic shift, economic transformation and resource scarcity. Our culture must put distractions and entertainments in their proper place, for the welfare of all.

THE CONTRADICTORY GUN CULTURE OF THE UNITED STATES

Like all Americans, my thoughts have been with the victims of the senseless, grisly tragedy in Aurora, Colorado. For the last few days, I have not felt like writing anything on the Internet until the initial wave of predictable nonsense gave way to some mental space. I simply haven't been in the mood to add to the reflexive cacophony of long-held opinions and election year blather. This moment is too sad for that, too predictable, too much of a goddamn waste. I have little to add to help appreciate the tragedy. Perhaps I can provide an atypical perspective from a little-known part of America.

As my friends and regular readers know, I hail originally from the state of Vermont, just like seven previous generations of my family. The Green Mountain State has come to be known for a great many things that are quaint and tourist friendly – Ben & Jerry's ice cream, skiing, the Vermont Teddy Bear Factory, Green Mountain Coffee, and "Larry, Darryl and Darryl," so long as you were watching television in the 1980s. One facet of Vermont life is neither famous nor quaint: *Vermonters are armed to the teeth*. Guns are absolutely everywhere. Rifles. Pistols. Shotguns. Muzzleloaders. Semiautomatics. 50 caliber tripod-mount "semi" automatics that could take out aircraft. Every firearm you can possibly imagine. Vermont could be the most armed part of the *world* per capita, as rife with firearms as Afghanistan, but with trees and cheddar cheese.

Why have you never heard of this crazy, paranoid armed madhouse? Because Vermont routinely has the lowest violent crime in the United States, with only Maine competing for the title of safest place – and it's armed to the teeth as well. Are you thinking, "*well, maybe Vermont has a lot of guns, but surely they have safe and sane gun control laws.*" Sorry – we have basically no limitations. Behold the most lax group of regulations you can imagine. There are no concealed carry laws – you can walk around with a trench coat loaded with shotguns, if that floats your boat. There are no open carry laws – feel free to shop for groceries looking like Dirty Harry with a .45 hand cannon strapped to your belt. There are no limits to the number of weapons you can own – if you have the cash, feel free to arm a militia with 3,000 handguns and hunting rifles. The list of gun rules are comically loose, even by American standards: it's a $200 fine for wearing a gun on the way to *kill someone* (?), a $50 fine for pointing a loaded weapon at someone other than for self-defense, and the only thing we're really straightforward on is not arming school children or bringing guns to court with you. The rules allow all kinds of guns, everywhere, and Vermonters thus purchase and own and bear all kinds of guns, everywhere.

And you never hear of massacres in Vermont. The state feels about as safe and wholesome as any place in the world, with thousands of tourists streaming in during winter skiing, summer camping and fall leaf-peeping with nary an idea that they are surrounded by the most armed populus in the United States. This is for two reasons, one obvious, and one a bit more complex and contradictory.

Guns don't kill people; economic inequality and suburbs do

The main reason that Vermont gets away with tons of firearms and no violence is that there is low population density and a low Gini coefficient. There aren't many people per square mile, and there's no huge rich poor gap. It's more like a poor-kinda poor-not-that-poor-gap, and it creates relatively little social tension. There is enough open space and secluded land for most Vermonters to live on their own private property with little friction with neighbors – excepting, of course, Town Meeting Day in March, which may result in hot debate of snow plow budgets, but which is rarely enough to cause much animosity. Compare this with parts of America where the rich, middle-class and terribly poor are constantly glaring at each other, part of the same tax base but not the same culture. I'm thinking specifically of my last two residences, Washington DC and Saint Louis – places where people are shooting each other in the hind end all of the time. Vermont has none of that tension, even though it has far more firearms.

The next reason that I give as to the relative lack of violent crime in Vermont will sound shockingly similar to NRA talking points, and will likely discomfit people thinking about the need for new gun laws in the wake of yet one more massacre abetted by easy access to firearms.In Vermont, you assume that everybody is armed and will shoot you if you mess with them.I don't mean that people shoot each other over Red Sox games or over simple neighborly disputes. But if you plan on approaching anybody at night or on their property with anything other than friendly intent, you risk being shot. The ubiquity of firearms – and people who damn well know how to use them – means that culturally, you have a lot of respect for property and privacy.

I learned my first lesson about this in high school. One of my high school classmates, James Ashcroft, was with several members of our basketball team as they went to steal liquor from the garage of Robert Bizon, a local bar owner at around 2:30 am. They did not know that he had been robbed so many times that he had placed an alarm inside his garage and announced to the community – including a variety of passersby at my father's farm store – that he was going to kill the next person to rip him off. When he came upon a gang of people on his property late at night, he shot Ashcroft and refused to call the paramedics for several minutes. He died at Rutland Hospital up the road a couple hours later.

Bizon was charged with involuntary manslaughter – and acquitted. I remember the community response. It's not that people weren't outraged and disgusted at the senseless death, the overreaction of somebody who seemed relish the opportunity to shoot whoever violated his property next – that was clearly ugly. But as a matter of culture many Vermonters in the area said, "*Well, don't go on people's land at 2:30 in the morning, up to no good.*" There was no push for a "James' Law," no attempt to blame guns. It was too bad. Then again, Vermont culture dictates that in the middle of the night, when five unidentified guys are lurking, you may not have the benefit of time to decide.

America needs more than one set of gun laws

I compare this culture with recent events. Let me just say that having lived in major cities, **I do not believe that America should just have one set of gun laws.** What works for Vermont – producing the lowest crime in the country – would be insane in Washington DC, which has the highest crime, around 1,400 rapes, murders or robberies per year per 100,000 residents – ten times the Vermont average. Do I want the residents of Northeast DC to have 50 caliber tripod rifles and armor piercing bullets? Does Saint Louis require yet more handguns, restricting firearms only at courthouses and schools? No, that's insanity.

The violence in America does not spring up around places of high firearm ownership, or Maine would look like Chechnya. Violence, and the most disturbing cases of deranged mass murder in recent years, having been springing up in locales with the poor and rich living side by side. The most perverse plans to murder people tend toward the suburbs, a state of living which lacks the realness and interdependence of either dense urban centers or diffuse agrarian regions. You are living too close to people about whom you couldn't care less. That, or in the case of places like West Baltimore and East St Louis, you are living in a place that is packed with people, but people do not work together toward a common goal, to stricken by the diseased lifestyle of poverty. This afflicted lifestyle occurs in a country where guns are easy to acquire, by legal or illegal means. Sick minds meet available ammunition. The mix is lethal.

Does America need new gun laws in the aftermath of the Aurora tragedy? I would say the answer is complex and contradictory. In one sense, no – because Vermont does not require new gun restriction, nor

Maine, nor Wyoming. But do the suburbs and cities require a dramatic restriction of firearms to reduce the number of people living in pathogenic suburban automobile slums or decayed urban wastelands from going crazy and taking out their fever dream on a crowded theater? My sense is yes. As a lifelong Vermont separatist, I think it is up to the local cities and states to make that decision.

Then again, maybe the problem isn't guns, but of a culture of consumerism, suburbanism, myth, delusion, disappointment, isolation and resentment. That is a much more difficult issue to legislate.

TALES FROM THE SOCIOPATHIC SOCIETY

My friend and colleague August Jackson tweets today regarding Jon Corzine's return to finance and Jonah Lehrer's maybe-maybe-not rehabilitation at WIRED magazine:

I wonder what it means, though, that we're not even going though the motions of contrition on anyone's part anymore.

Personally, I think it means that our most cherished institutions are in the process of extinction. The elites running these institutions, occupiers of very privileged positions at the top of our socioeconomic pyramid, are not even bothering to maintain the values that are supposed to underlie their legitimacy. They are letting their myths come apart, tattered sails torn asunder by winds from all directions. It means a great number of things: arrogance, sociopathy, but most of all – the end of their particular dynasty.

The myth of the competent elite

All throughout industrial society we have a myth of the "competent elite" that separates our society from the "feudal dictators" of yore. The myth tells us, in the Bad Old Days, people were above you in society because of who their parents were. You gave your labor to provide for their luxury for no other reason other than threat of force if you did not comply. So continues the myth, in the Good Old Days of Today people may be above you in society, but this is because they are competent, deserving of their wealth, and doing more for society as a whole than some lesser deserving, less competent person might.

We have, on the whole, gone out of our way to protect this myth. The Japanese, most famously, mixed their bushido culture into this set of beliefs, and will occasionally jump off buildings by way of apology for a failure to meet the levels of competence expected in modern organizations.They at the very least resign in shame after a rigorous period of *sumimasen* public apology.

A Chinese colleague told me recently, "Had a Chinese CEO led any bank to what all of your banks did in concert, his bonus package would have been a bullet to the temple."

Even the French, originators of recognizable terms such as *aristocratie*, *dauphin* and *buffoon,* as well as inventors of white powdery wigs for rich folk, even they are careful to maintain appearances. When French President Nicolas Sarkozy's son Jean Sarkozy was suggested as the head of EPAD, the economic region of *La Défense* just west of Paris, the French went into revolt. The President's son was only 23 years old, still in college, and this would be roughly like putting him in charge of economic development of all Manhattan, with a billion dollars of budget a year at his disposal. The public forced father and son to reconsider such an audacious proposal. The French don't always receive competence from their bureaucrats, but with their belief in elite schools like Polytechnique and ENA, they sure expect it – and reject any return to hereditary aristocracy. (Any more than they already have, of course.)

America: where it's OK to not say sorry

Which brings us to America. We have a sociopathic trend of apologizing for nothing, even when it hurts millions of people.

Has a single Wall Street CEO apologized for causing chaos?

Has any supporter of the war in Iraq come forth to apologize for leading the country on a misguided, terribly managed bloodbath based on laughably false intelligence?

Has George Lucas personally begged forgiveness for Jar Jar Binks, and that terrible whiny scene of Darth Vader going, "PADMEEEEEEEEEE... PADMEEEEEE?"

Has anyone from Penn State apologized for creating a culture that allowed child rape to flourish in its football program – without griping about Paterno's statue or their goddamn past football record?

You don't even get ashamed silence from these cretins – you get bailed-out Wall Street CEOs complaining about Obama's socialism, new hedge funds from guys like Corzine, pretensions of victimhood from college football fans.

But why?

I think that you hold your values dear when you are looking at the future. Your systems work, your institutions are in tact, and personal pride cannot get in the way of a functional future.

When you *aren't* looking at the future, because deep inside you know that you belong to an obsolete dynasty, then you throw caution to the wind. Why apologize? I should get mine. Let the others apologize. Because there is no tomorrow.

YOUR WELL-REGULATED MILITIA WILL NOT KICK ANYBODY'S ASS

I am the father of two children. I picked them both up at daycare after work this evening.

Tonight, there are fathers in Connecticut who could not pick up their children because they were dead. This is because there was yet one more massacre by another lunatic without a prefrontal cortex who decided to get out his angst toward society by availing himself of our copiously available assault weapons.

I am from Vermont, a state that is armed to the teeth. We have the lowest crime in America. I grew up around weapons. My family has guns. I am a crack shot. I do not demonize weaponry. Also, I have no use for firearms in my day-to-day adult life.

As of today, witnessing two mass murders this week, I have had it with people suggesting that allowing the completely unfettered availability of small arms is essential to the operation of a modern democracy. You are not going to preserve democracy through the availability of your deadly-yet-inconsequential assault weaponry. You are only increasingly the likelihood of miscreants murdering our children or random people at malls.

I know you don't like this. I don't care anymore.

The roots of your fantasy

I am a fully traditional American, and I understand the myth of the American revolution. Yes, an armed population took on the largest imperial force in the world back in the late 18th century. (We only won because of the French wanting to screw with their main global rivals, but it still counts.) And let's examine, just briefly, the armaments that went into that victory:

English assets

- Guys with muskets
- Guys with cannons
- Guys with frigates

American assets

- Guys with muskets
- Home field advantage
- Whisky
- Squirrel meat

Pretty even match up, wouldn't you say? Our infantry was roughly equivalent, though the British regulars were (as opposed to American myth) way, way better trained. The Limeys had more money, less knowledge of the terrain, and, only at the end, the French Empire funding their opponents, so they walked away in favor of India, South Africa, and other, more profitable adventures. The Colonists should have lost, but fate intervened.

As a result, Americans maintain the belief that they will still be able to reform and/or defeat government on its soil using "The Second Amendment." This clause of the Bill of Rights makes way for Americans to maintain armaments much in the same spirit of 1775, such that its citizens might once again rise up with muskets whenever necessary to Defeat Tyranny on Their Soil.

There is one major problem with this dangerously outdated assumption: the chasm between government weaponry and civilian weaponry is comically large. Like, *from here to Venus* large. So large that your defense of arming every schizophrenic and bipolar douchebag with AR-15s because you want to "*prevent tyranny from taking root*" is absurdly, ridiculously stupid.

Oh, you think you have a shot at overthrowing The Current American Government? Really? Well let's backtrack.

Your odds of taking back America with an over-under shotgun

Before I get to the weapons comparison, let's just get on the same page about something. If you're a libertarian conservative type and you enjoy the idea of overthrowing tyranny with your hunting rifles, the last decade has been something of a clusterfuck. If your dream of dreams is personally overthrowing a misguided totalitarian militarist regime, well, you've been headed in the wrong goddamn direction.

Since those nineteen barbarian asswipes from the Middle East used our own technology to murder 3000 of our citizens, the American Military Industrial Complex has been on a bit of a rampage. The Patriot Act. The Department of Homeland Security. Total Information Awareness. Iraq. Afghanistan. Baghram. Guantanamo. Enhanced Interrogation. Satellites, reading your email, backscatter scans at the airport, dickheads feeling in your wife's underwear band. Yeah, there sure are a lot of unchecked federal government security operations these days because a few Arabs snuck one by the goalie.

Problem is, there were a whole lot of people in America who cheered for this crap, and tragically, they are the same people who claim they want freedom from the Gubmint. It's pretty hard to argue for a weak government at home when you want it strong enough to invade Mesopotamia. Either way – we have funded and cheerled a very, very strong federal military apparatus with the power to project its volition all over the globe.

OK, let us take a step back and assume that you, on the Thursday of your choosing, decide that you would like to break the bonds between your holy territory in Dogballs, Arkansas, and the Federal Gubmint in Washington DC. And you are planning on using, in the words of our great stateswoman, Sarah Palin, "Second Amendment solutions."

AWESOME! LET'S GET IT ON!!! And let's do a quick comparison between what you, the aging suburbanite have, versus the current American Armed Forces, battled hardened in Mazar-e-Sharif and Fallujah after 50 years of major R&D.

WEAPONRY AVAILABLE TO THE AMERICAN CITIZENRY

What kinds of nasty toys will you bring to bear against the Military-Industry Complex when you've had enough and decide to get filled up with bourbon and gumption?

Bushmaster M4 Patrolman

Caliber: 5.56mm or .223 Rem.
Magazine Capacity: 30 Rounds (accepts all M16 type)
Overall Length: 34.75" [88.27 cm]
Length – Stock Retracted: 32.5″ [82.55 cm]

Ruger SR22 Pistol

Slide Material: Aluminum
Slide Finish: Black Anodize
Grip Frame: Black Polymer
Sights: Adjustable 3-Dot
Barrel Length: 3.50″
Overall Length: 6.40″
Height: 4.90″
Width:1.29″

Zastava PAP AK-47 Copy

Features:

- *7.62x39mm caliber*
- *stamped receiver*
- *hinged top cover*
- *weighs 5.69 lbs.*
- *comes with two hi-cap magazines*
- *Maximum range – > 500 yards; effective range- < 300 yards*

OK, all set with what The American People will be playing with? Let's move onto the more interesting set, the toys of the Rogue State that we are supposed to oppose with our Second Amendment Solution!

WEAPONRY AVAILABLE TO THE UNITED STATES ARMED FORCES

M-1 Abrams Tank

The **M1 Abrams** is a third-generation main battle tank produced in the United States. Highly mobile, designed for modern armored ground warfare, the M1 is well armed and heavily armored. Notable features include the use of a powerful gas turbine engine (multifuel capable, usually fueled with JP8 jet fuel), the adoption of sophisticated composite armor, and separate ammunition storage in a blowout compartment for crew safety. Weighing nearly 68 short tons (almost 62 metric tons), it is one of the heaviest main battle tanks in service.

Active protection system

In addition to the armor, some Abrams are equipped with a Softkill Active protection system, the AN/VLQ-6 Missile Countermeasure Device (MCD) that can impede the function of guidance systems of some semi-active control line-of-sight (SACLOS) wire and radio guided anti-tank missiles (such as the Russian AT-3, AT-4, AT-5, AT-6 and the like) and thermally and infrared guided missiles.[42] The MCD works by emitting a massive, condensed infrared signal to confuse the seeker of an anti-tank guided missile (ATGM). However, the drawback to the system is that the ATGM is not destroyed, it is merely directed away from its intended target, leaving the missile to detonate elsewhere. This device is mounted on the turret roof in front of the loader's hatch, and can lead some people to mistake Abrams fitted with these devices for the M1A2 version, since the Commander's Independent Thermal Viewer on the latter is mounted in the same place, though the MCD is box-shaped and fixed in place as opposed to cylindrical and rotating like the CITV.

Armor

The Abrams is protected by armor based on the British-designed Chobham armor, a further development of the British 'Burlington' armor. Chobham is a composite armor formed by spacing multiple layers of various alloys of steel, ceramics, plastic composites, and kevlar, giving an estimated maximum (frontal turret) 1,320–1,620 millimetres (52–64 in) of RHAe versus HEAT (and other chemical energy rounds) and 940–960 mm (37–38 in) versus kinetic energy penetrators. It may also be fitted with reactive armor over the track skirts if needed (as in the Urban Survival Kit) and slat armor over the rear of the tank and rear fuel cells to protect against ATGMs. Protection against spalling is provided by a Kevlar liner. Beginning in 1987, M1A1 tanks received improved armor packages that incorporated depleted uranium (DU) mesh in their armor at the front of the turret and the front of the hull. Armor reinforced in this manner offers significantly increased resistance towards all types of anti-tank weaponry, but at the expense of adding considerable weight to the tank, as depleted uranium is 1.7 times more dense than lead.

Boeing AH-64 Apache

The **Boeing AH-64 Apache** is a four-blade, twin-engine attack helicopter with a tailwheel-type landing gear arrangement, and a tandem cockpit for a two-man crew.

The AH-64 Apache features a nose-mounted sensor suite for target acquisition and night vision systems. It is armed with a30-millimeter (1.2 in) M230 Chain Gun carried between the main landing gear, under the aircraft's forward fuselage. It has four hardpoints mounted on stub-wing pylons, typically carrying a mixture of AGM-114 Hellfire missiles and Hydra 70 rocket pods. The AH-64 has a large amount of systems redundancy to improve combat survivability.

One of the revolutionary features at the introduction of the Apache was its helmet mounted display, the Integrated Helmet and Display Sighting System (IHADSS); among other abilities the pilot or gunner can slave the helicopter's 30 mm automatic M230 Chain Gun to his helmet, making the gun track head movements to point at where he looks. The M230E1 can be alternatively fixed to a locked forward firing position, or controlled via the Target Acquisition and Designation System (TADS). The AH-64′s standard of performance for aerial gunnery is to achieve at least one hit out of 30 shots fired at a wheeled vehicle 800–1200 m away

Tactical nuclear weapons

Okay, enough said.

You are better off writing blog posts

Can we get real here? You are not going to defeat the United States Military. At all.

Are you thinking that if the system of governance in the United States doesn't suit you, it is always a possibility to use your stockpiled AK-47 ripoffs to force a new rule of law at the point of a gun after a few years, just like back in 1776?

No fucking way.

How are you going to organize? Government agents can monitor your email, search engine requests, Facebook communications, and phone calls if they have any reason to worry about you.

Are you going to attack military facilities? Really? Are you going to hide in the hills? In the cities? Are you going to face down Seal Team Six, which dealt with Osama bin Laden deep inside of Pakistan? With a few bottle rockets? Honestly?

If you want change, *you are better off writing poems*. The notion of taking on a military that is unchallenged in the world is utterly absurd.

Write about justice. Think about peace. Argue for economic opportunity. All good things.

Fight for smaller government. Start all the libertarian blogs you want.

But cut it out with the nonsense that making assault weapons available to all of North America does something other than provide schizophrenics with props for their murder fantasies. Because you aren't George Washington, or Nathaniel Green, or Patrick Henry. You are somebody wondering when the next mass murderer is going to invade a daycare.

Just like I am.

THOUGHTS ON POST-POSTMODERN BUSINESS MANAGEMENT

The interesting thing about all of the changes described above is that the business world tends to act like things are fundamentally stable. Growth shall return when customers get back to their credit cards and start spending for Christmas, amiright?

America's ingrained business techniques, ironically called "best practices" are often far too slow to change to be useful in this new world. Here are a few weaknesses I have spotted, and ways I think our businesses can adapt to the world after Normal.

GETTING EXECUTIVE BUY-IN IS A SHAM

It seems that every conference I ever went to on intelligence, foresight or research had a track about "how to get executive buy-in" or "how to get a seat at the table" or "winning over the C-suite." Today, I saw an article on this topic for the 95,000th time, and it occurred to me to finally crystalize my point of view on this.

Stop trying to win over the C-suite, you are wasting your time. And definitely stop give classes, webinars, and conference tracks on how to do so.

Here's why.

If we are going to generalize about executives as if they are all interchangeable – and lord knows, that is most of business literature – then there are only two ways to win the confidence of top executives:

1. Do a very good job for many people in the organization over a long period of time, such that your work is perceived to be trustworthy by people up and down the hierarchy.

2. Tell the executives what they already believe.

You can't teach the first point, and nobody really wants to discuss the psychology behind the second point.

Building your brand is a matter of competence and a matter of politics. First, you must be able to do your job as a researcher and analyst competently. This is within your power. However, making this politically popular is not up to you. It really depends on the culture and climate of your organization, and whether people really *like* somebody running around, analyzing the world well and delivering insightful implications about what it means for top management. And if you are not in an organization that likes that sort of thing, then forget about brand building, ***get a new job***. You can do an exceptional job at an organization full of stupid political hacks – *I have experience in this matter* – and you still are not going to "win the C-suite." You're going to end up with your desk next to the boiler in the basement, or out in the parking lot.

The other way to reliably win access to C-Suite is to be a consummate butt kisser and consistently bend your analysis in whatever direction the prevailing political winds are blowing. The best way to assure "executive buy-in" is to show up with information that supports past decisions and existing biases. To be sure, you'll need the veneer of data to support your findings – *we're all professionals, of course* – and if that data flatters top executives rather than challenges them, you can plan on return visits to the comfy chairs in the room with the really nice table.

Here's why intelligence is constantly begging for approval

A follow-up question to ask is "*why are we constantly pleading for top executives to take intelligence seriously?*" As I mentioned, I have seen this conference track at close to a million conferences for over a billion years, and never is it asked, "*Jeez, why are people in the information field constantly begging for acceptance?*" You would think that in these modern organizations full of managers with master's degrees, the thirst for scientific evidence behind decisions would be unquenchable. But here we are, every year, professionals talking amongst themselves about how to get those elusive "c-suite executives" to finally take intelligence seriously.

The reality of the situation is that most managers see intelligence as a way to justify a decision that is already made, not to learn something new. At the end of the day, intelligence serves decision makers – and the people involved in intelligence are rarely at a peer level in the organization. This means that from the word go, intelligence professionals are in a subservient position, and are often judged for how their work output makes people look and feel. When they make people look or feel bad – which fresh information about the outside world often can – intelligence professionals take a beating in terms of reputation.

It's not fair. It's not pretty. Then again, isn't the intelligence field supposed to be about reality as opposed to comfortable assumptions? Good. Then we can all accept this point and stop writing about the magic formula to be loved by top executives. The truth is simple and a bit ugly.

THE POSH, PREDICTABLE WORLD OF BUSINESS CONFERENCES

Nucky Thompson is proving David Denby right. The *New Yorker* movie critic recently declared in a brilliant, erudite cultural analysis that Hollywood has killed the movie as a medium, abandoning audiences looking for quality in favor of endless superheroes battling obviously fake CGI monsters. Television, long derided as a more proletarian medium, is unexpectedly becoming the only place for dense, intelligent drama, and incisive comedy. After watching a few recent episodes of HBO's *Boardwalk Empire*, I thought about how right Denby was. Steve Buscemi's portrayal of antihero mob kingpin Nucky Thompson is the stuff you almost never see on the big screen anymore — extraordinarily deep character development, moral dilemma, actions, consequences, and a human drama as rich as life itself. Try getting that out of the endless string of superhero films or "franchise reboots" that slouch out of Tinseltown these days.

Which brings me to business conferences, oddly enough. While ruminating on the limitations of the medium and business model of film, my mind drifted to another channel for content that ought to be exciting and enriching, but is often just as shallow and bombastic as Hollywood — the timeworn ritual of annual conferences. Just as TV was thought to be frivolous and film serious, social media has a reputation as mere entertainment while business conferences are serious, important events.

Lately, though, conferences have been big budget but formulaic, while the quality discussions appear to be online, a place where cute cat videos and pictures of people's breakfast once reigned. The paradigm is shifting in favor of new technology and new ways of relating.

Doesn't it seem like conferences are almost identical no matter where you go and for no matter which industry? First there's location — if you want to meet your colleagues face to face, you are likely to end up in Chicago, Philadelphia, London, Orlando (God forbid) or any place with a sufficiently large conference hall, hotel and airport hub. People all huddle in a lightless, airless building the size of an airplane hangar. There is the obligatory gigantic vendor space, with everyone standing in front of identical booths that are reminiscent of high school science projects. Plenary sessions feature the same welcomes as last year, possibly adjusted for any financial crises that may or may not be going on. Breakout sessions feature vendors and consultants barely hiding sales pitches within presentations. The evening keynote is either an author recycling his conclusions from an old book, a sport hero, or a retired executive from a famous company. By the final day, people meander through the conference hall, avoiding the gaze of tired, blathering sales people in the vendor booths. Three days and several thousands of dollars per person later, people return home with a stack of business cards and their fundamental assumptions still sadly intact.

Nothing dramatic goes down at a conference, for the most part. There are no major polemics on stage. No shocking news is unveiled. The keynoter does not provoke a response positive or negative in the attendees. The event coordinators hold their breath and hope nothing unplanned happens, and usually, it doesn't.

Meanwhile, on Twitter, LinkedIn, Google+, or wherever, people are free to unveil outrageous proposals, fight it out on comment streams, make common cause through private messages, learn, absorb, disagree, and generally participate in a vigorous intellectual process. It's not that online communities are always this way, nor that live conferences are always stultifying — but million-dollar conferences are usually thought of as too precious to involve risk and adventure. They are like Hollywood — big budget and totally predictable.

I love seeing people face to face. There is no substitute in the digital space for actual human contact. But if we're going to burn millions of gallons of petroleum and spend thousands of bucks for a ticket, shouldn't we expect something more exciting, unpredictable, or enriching?

What if your industry had a conference and did not announce the schedule or the speakers until people showed up on site?

What if you let people elect the speakers once they got to the conference?

What if the keynote was given by your industry's most vociferous critic, who allowed ample time for Q&A to fight it out with the participants?

What if you brought three thousand people to a congress and changed the name and purpose of the group before you left at the end of the week?

What if you met and decided that your professional society needed to separate into two different organizations before you walked out?

What if a conference included a 33% chance of a scandal emerging?

I'll tell you what — if any of this was possible, I would be more likely to lay out $1,499 for the ticket. It might be fun.

Or we could all just swap business cards at the cocktail hour.

WHAT HAPPENS WHEN THERE'S NO GROWTH TO MANAGE

The 1980s and 1990s was an unprecedented period of economic expansion in the United States. America doubled down on a strategy of suburbs, automobiles, housing, and the debt-fueled trappings of a consumer economy, which worked like gangbusters, boosting GDP for the nation, creating millions of jobs, and swelling corporate profits left and right. Not surprisingly, thousands of business books by American authors were translated into dozens of languages so that business students around the world could learn from what came to be known as "best practices."

Lately, of course, the old magic seems to be gone. Corporate profits have been doing fine so far, but U.S.-style corporate management seems to be leading in an unproductive direction. Standards of living are falling, jobs are hard to come by, and national coffers are empty. Meanwhile several industries are caught smack in the middle of major disruptions — media, retail, and automotive, just to name a few.

In other words, the best practices developed during the booming '80s and '90s, taught in MBA programs around the world, and liberally applied to industry after industry might be based on outdated assumptions. A look at a few different macroeconomic trend lines suggests that maybe we need to rethink a few things.

We need to ask if a significant portion of MBA thinking is based on a faulty assumption that global GDP will keep growing in perpetuity. Perhaps the growth we experienced in recent decades was based on a few extraordinary conditions.

I originally got this idea from energy analyst Gregor MacDonald, who was asked why economists seemed so slow to include world energy markets in any of their assumptions. Gregor replied that policies developed in a time when energy inputs got cheaper every year were not very useful these days, because the effect of more expensive energy inputs was basically unthinkable.

It's not like nobody ever thought about energy inputs before. Benjamin Franklin created the efficient Franklin stove on the grounds of national security. To be economically and militarily safe, he reasoned, America needed to protect its energy assets — forests and firewood! But people whose formative years go from 1985 to 1999 might have been seduced by the belief that cheap energy was a permanent fixture.

What are some other assumptions managers might not be examining when making strategy? Let's take a look at retail, the cornerstone of the 20th century consumer economy. Even after the crash of 2008, I heard many executives in the U.S. predicting a return to growth in the suburban big box retail space. It was unthinkable to them that this model was broken. Yet the U.S. has vastly more retail space than other wealthy nations — over 23 square feet per person, compared with to 3.3 in Sweden and 2.3 in France, a country that pioneered the department store with Printemps and Galéries Lafayette. Many American executives have argued that America is physically larger, and so retail will continue to grow. But the trends say otherwise. We're now at a fraction of the retail space growth of the last four decades.

Then there's housing, that great driver of consumerism, the center of the American Dream that *The Atlantic* recently reported isn't on the radar of younger generations. The drop off in new housing completions is precipitous — beyond the boom and bust cycle of prior decades.

But wait, this is just cyclical, right? Surely the next generation of consumers, The Millennials, will reach the right age and begin buying like its 1987!

Yeah, about that. First, there's never been a generation in so much debt. And moreover, it is not like the job market is rising to meet Millennials to help them pay off that record debt. It's like the recession of 1980, only with billions more in school loans and maxed credit cards.

There are tons of stats showing we're in a brand new world. Generations of MBAs have been following a playbook that teaches how to lead a company in times of unprecedented growth. If the model for growth has changed — perhaps permanently — shouldn't this be a moment to reconsider management techniques? There is plenty to discuss.

GLOBAL ECONOMIC COMPETITION IN THE TWILIGHT OF THE NATION-STATE

Harvard Business School professor Michael Porter wants to make America competitive again. This would be an insanely ambitious project for anyone, but then again we are talking about the person who singlehandedly invented the modern concept of business competition. As this article in Fortune details, Porter actually invented the majority of the language we use to describe the behavior of two or more firms serving the same kinds of customers. We could not describe the complex dance between companies, customers, suppliers and competitors before Porter offered a general theory of competitive dynamics. His models were so predictive that his language has been adopted in every business school in the world, and is now even applied to the notion of economic competition between nations. Now, he and his colleagues at HBS are applying those ideas to the real-world issues facing America's ability to compete – high unemployment, declining wages, financial instability, fewer small businesses being started. The solution to this will be encouraging businesses to compete in such a way that creates shared value, enduring investments on American soil that create a virtuous circle of prosperity.

As an American, naturally I'm pulling for this effort to be successful. But in thinking a bit longer about the proposition, I am concerned about a potential problem: I'm not certain that nation-states, as discrete actors, can really compete anymore in the Porterian sense. The emergence of transnational corporate structures and complex, tightly interwoven global financial markets has compromised the units of analysis we use for competition. Moreover, the state of politics makes it unlikely that a shared value initiative could emerge if it countered the interests of powerful corporations who have a more influential voice than ever in the formation of policy. Nation-states as institutions are not in a state of competition so much as a state of complex cooperation. This cooperation is insufficiently understood and may even be the source of some of our woes.

Our current definitions prevent useful analysis

First, we have the problem of defining the nation-state in 2012 and describing how it should act as a competitor. Capital structure, supply chains and global markets compromise the independence of nation-states, making it exceedingly difficult to view them as separate entities that compete discretely. This may sound counterintuitive. China makes solar panels, the U.S. makes solar panels; they compete to see who can sell the most. But global commerce may be somewhat more complex than it was in the 1980s and 90s when we started using this language. The liberalization of trade and the development of an elaborate global financial system has meant a historic growth in GDP and shared material prosperity that is unprecedented; one can also argue that it prevents war. Yet this global integration of commerce has also led our institutions to become intertwined to a degree that makes describing their behavior increasingly tricky.

Modern capital structure, though offering new opportunities for global collaboration, also compromises the discrete nature of national competitors. As an example, Citibank is an American firm, and a strategically important one at that due to its unprecedented size. Its success is in nominally in the interest of the nation known as the United States of America. The nation protects Citibank, offering it billions in bailout funds when the firm's own risk management is insufficient, just as it did in 2008. Naturally, this distorts the financial services market, picking winners, stifling the process of creative destruction and offering perverse incentives for risky behavior – but the fate of the nation is supposedly on the line. So what do we make of the fact that 25% of Citibank is owned by investment holding companies from Abu Dhabi, Singapore, and Saudi Arabia? The U.S. government protects a corporation's interests through bailouts, but also protects the financial investment of other countries at the same time. And at no time is it clear what Citibank owes back to the nation-state aside taxes – which they will assiduously avoid.

To see the further complexity imposed by our global supply chains, take the case of Apple. Looking at the future of U.S. competition, surely we want the giant of Cupertino, California to succeed even more than it already has. But then, the way the company's operations are set up, jobs in America might not flourish the way that the balance sheet would. After all, the manufacturing is happening over at Foxconn in Shenzhen, China. So we can't say that Apple's competitiveness will mean America wins and China loses; it's more of a partnership. But surely we can apply the competitive model to Apple versus Korea's Samsung electronics. But then

Samsung uses Chinese manufacturing too. So it seems that China wins in either case, and neither Korea nor the U.S. can compete "against" the Middle Kingdom for this branch of consumer electronics. It's much more of a partnership all around.

The globalization of markets further blurs the lines between nations attempting to compete through private firms. A great many of America's most successful corporations take an increasingly global outlook, by which their success is not tied to any one nation-state. From pharmaceuticals to soft drinks to automobiles, most major competitors in America (and elsewhere) have their eyes firmly fixed on revenue growth in Brazil, evolving consumer tastes in India, the rising Middle Class of China. Many corporations are quite agnostic when it comes to choosing a home country, as recently witnessed when Boeing made noises about moving its headquarters to China – an unusual suggestion for a critical military contractor. And where tax liability is concerned, all companies of such size employ accountants who can skillfully position cash flow so as to minimize what they owe back to their home nation-state in taxation. Basically, for many of America's corporations, the competitiveness of the United States in and of itself is an ancillary issue in a much larger business strategy.

Are "the people" willing or able to defend national interests?

Herein lies a major problem in the search for national competitiveness: America's largest businesses are beholden to shareholders far more than they are to the citizens of the nation. In fact, corporate executives bear the legal burden of fiduciary responsibility to the companies they lead – but not to the nation in which live, not to their neighbors. They are fully expected to maximize profit for their employer in the short-term. No CEO would last five minutes if he or she announced that they were going to take a loss this year because they hired 1000 people in Detroit to help out a great American city facing hard times. No Board of Directors would tolerate a CFO who decided not to rout cash flow through the Irish subsidiary first, deciding instead to recognize the income in this fiscal year because, well, somebody's got to deal with America's deficit problem. This is not to say that corporations are, by definition, unwilling to produce shared value, but it is undeniable that failing to benefit stakeholders is a whole lot less damaging than failing to meet earning expectations on the Street.

This would suggest that the American people must form a movement for national competitiveness, a political consciousness to shape markets through regulation in order to achieve broadly shared value – improving standards of living, better economic opportunity, and a vibrant civil society. There is only one problem with that: with recent help from the Citizens United Supreme Court decision, America's corporations can intervene directly in the election of individuals who would seek to regulate them. How are the American people supposed to advance this agenda of national competitiveness through policy, when the very corporations they hope to change can finance individual politicians' campaigns? How can there be a dialogue between government and business when one finances the other?

And aside from direct campaign finance, lobbying has become a multimillion dollar enterprise which allows corporations first and best access to lawmakers any time they reveal any potential legislation that could change the competitive landscape in America. Recall the avalanche of money poured in over Medicare Part D legislation and the Affordable Care Act. Healthcare represents a crippling 17% of U.S. GDP, 50% more expenditure than the next comparable nation. These two attempts to modify the pharmaceutical and health insurance industries were met with unprecedented amounts of lobbying; there were 1248 organizations lobbying to alter the Affordable Care Act alone, two and a half lobbyists for every member of Congress.

So if the American citizenry can't express their desire for national competitiveness through federal government policies, why would companies beholden to shareholders move in that direction? It is not to say that they couldn't – but what is the business case for shared value investments? What, aside from the general enlightenment and presumed national pride of executives, would incentivize this behavior?

In their January 2011 Harvard Business Review article "Creating Shared Value," Michael Porter and Mark Kramer posit that capitalism is in crisis. I disagree on the grounds that the oligopolistic American economy is no longer particularly capitalistic. It's mercantilism that is in crisis. Our current business environment looks suspiciously like the economics of Adam Smith's day when he wrote The Wealth of Nations. By neglecting the spirit of its antitrust legislation in the past two decades, America has allowed its industries to become dangerously concentrated, from media to pharmaceuticals to – most harmfully – finance. Because of their size, they operate under an implicit guarantee from the U.S. government to be bailed out rather than be allowed to fail, taking jobs and tax base with them. Their size then allows them to obtain special benefits from the government in the form of subsidies, trade policies, and even deferred prosecutions.

The inherent inability of such a system to create shared value ("the wealth of nations") is what inspired Smith to push against mercantile companies with special privileges from the Crown in favor of small companies. A greater number of smaller firms, according to Smith, would be unable to lobby for special favors from the king, would be forced to innovate through competition, and would depend more on shared wealth in an ecosystem of communities rather than just concentrate money in a few well-connected hands. And such a competitive system would take care of itself, an "invisible hand" if you will. Perhaps this dynamic between large compromised economic institutions and free market innovators is really on one long cycle, as this argument seems surprisingly fresh today.

Thought leaders are having a sudden change of heart

It is interesting in 2012 to return to a nostalgia for the nation-state as the cradle of economic advantage, since many economists, business executives and politicians have been relentless in convincing the world that nations are essentially meaningless, an impediment to growth. To suggest the defense of national interest in the form of trade barriers or penalties to countries outsourcing jobs was to be accused of returning to the days of Smoot-Hawley, damning the world to economic depression.

Thomas Friedman travels the globe telling audiences that CEOs can now send their job anywhere in the world, so people should be "special" and do "extra." Also, he says that the globalization of jobs and the race to the bottom of wages is inevitable and that people should, "Do unto others before it is done unto them." He claims that this process will bring us to "small town values."

Financial Times journalist Martin Wolf, in his 2004 book *Why Globalization Works*, extolled the unqualified success of globalized markets and painted dissenters who worried about the risk to national fortunes as wild-eyed college radicals.

Australian mining magnate Gina Rinehart, the world's richest woman, recently warned Aussie miners that their demands for wage increases would make her business (which has recently seen iron ore commodity prices increase 881%) impossible to run, because Africans are willing to work for just $2 dollars a day.

Many Western thought leaders have been effusive in their support for these post-national structures, and business leadership has followed along both happily and profitably. To suddenly switch back to a national approach will be really rather a shock, both intellectually and practically. Imagine Wal-Mart, General Electric and Apple transitioning back to a primarily American strategy. Would such a course of action even be logistically or financially possible?

Moving forward instead of back

We are in a bind. The industrial West has begun transitioning to the next generation of political structures while retaining the myths and bureaucracies of the existing, moribund system. Our commercial efforts have already begun operating in a networked, post-national environment, where corporations have many homes and supernational institutions like the Euro bind together unlikely countrymen from Portugal to Greece. Yet, when banks and currencies threaten insolvency, our political leaders appeal to our sense of national security in asking for bailouts of "our" institutions. These inconsistencies lead to major political conflict that are currently being expressed in the streets of Athens, Madrid and Rome, but may spread.

Socially, our nations are divided by geography, ethnicity and language, though increasingly our real economic and social relationships are executed online, irrespective of the symbols written on our passports. Think of the number of people doing knowledge work at home for companies with clients all over the world who have no economic connection to their neighbors other than shopping at the same grocery store. Even more postmodern, think of people in China playing World of Warcraft professionally for Westerners who want their characters to be "leveled-up" while they sleep. With whom do these people share most in common?

Even cultural events are compromised. Take this years "politically charged" match between FC Barcelona and Real Madrid, a symbol of intra-national conflict that was in reality fought between Argentinians, Brazilians, Cameroonians and Spaniards who have little to do with Catalan secession or Castilian federalism. Well then, surely the nation-state can at least be defined by the fact that it builds and maintains its own physical infrastructure. But then you see that Arab investors own part of Chicago's parking meters and an Australian-Spanish partnership now operates the Indiana Toll Road. The list of post-national developments goes on.

To reach national competitiveness we would need to agree on what a nation is, what it is supposed to achieve, and how to improve results. That may be too far gone. It may be much more feasible to understand the state of new social, economic and cultural networks and learn how to leverage those in order to make the world just, healthy and prosperous. There is enormous amounts of intellectual work to be done on this matter, from redesigning taxation to determining the rights and obligations of citizens and corporations alike, to considering how to provide healthcare and national security in a shifting environment. These things are all within the range of possible, but the major competitive challenge will be in which group of people arrives first at a compelling narrative as to what's next - and what to do about it.

ABOUT THE AUTHOR

ERIC GARLAND is a writer, speaker, trend analyst, occasional TV talking head, bassist, linguist and freelance intellectual combatant who deals with the megatrends that affect society, economics and national security, with a special focus on what everyday people must do in a rapidly changing world. He is a contributor to The Atlantic, Harvard Business Review, Al Jazeera English, Russia Today, Huffington Post, and many other media outlets.

He is probably in a guitar store as you read this.

OTHER BOOKS BY ERIC GARLAND

Future Inc: How Businesses Can Anticipate and Profit from What's Next (AMACOM, 2007)

How to Predict the Future...and what to do about it so you WIN!!! (Wallingford Press, 2011)

www.ericgarland.co

58137275R00130

Made in the USA
Middletown, DE
19 December 2017